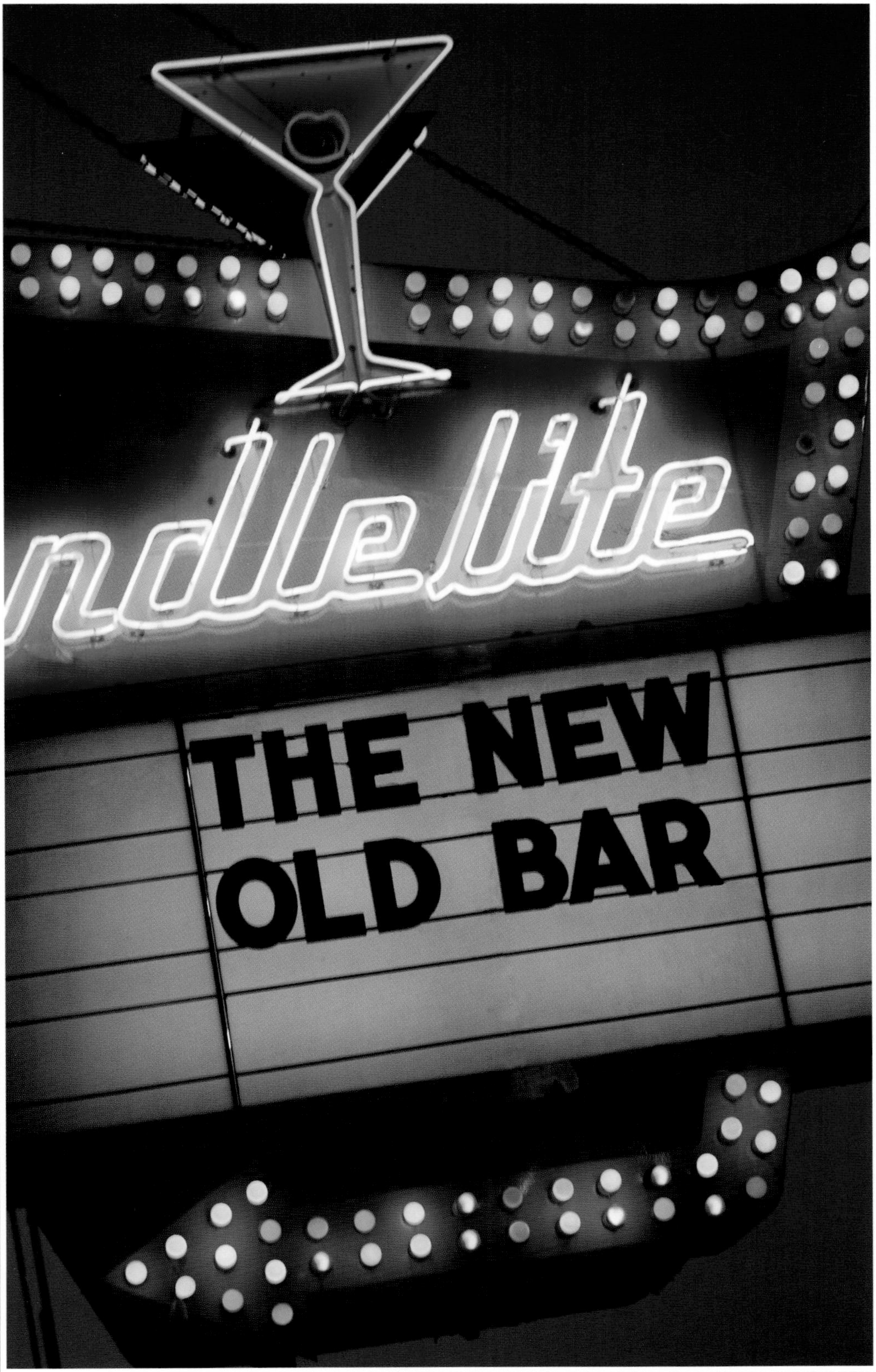
ndle lite
THE NEW
OLD BAR

THE NEW OLD BAR

CLASSIC COCKTAILS *and* **SALTY SNACKS**
from **THE HEARTY BOYS**

STEVE McDONAGH *and* DAN SMITH

PHOTOGRAPHY BY STEVE McDONAGH

MIDWAY

AN AGATE IMPRINT

CHICAGO

Printed in China.

All photography copyright © 2012 Steve McDonagh, except photographs on pages 5, 7, 12, 15, 23, 41, 153, 187, 203, 208 copyright © 2012 Bob Moysan.

Library of Congress Cataloging-in-Publication Data

McDonagh, Steve, 1964-

 The new old bar : classic cocktails and salty snacks from the hearty boys / Steve McDonagh and Dan Smith

    pages cm

 Summary: "A compendium for the home bar, including classic cocktail recipes, small plate recipes, mixology how-to's, and ingredient and equipment guides"-- Provided by publisher.

 Includes index.

 ISBN-13: 978-1-57284-139-0 (pbk.)

 ISBN-10: 1-57284-139-7 (flexibound)

 ISBN-13: (invalid) 978-1-57284-710-1 (ebook)

 1. Cocktails. 2. Snack foods. I. Title.

 TX951.M346 2012

 641.87'4--dc23

 2012022559

 10 9 8 7 6 5 4 3 2 1

Surrey Books is an imprint of Agate Publishing. Agate books are available in bulk at discount prices. For more information, go to agatepublishing.com.

Cautiously dedicated to our son, Nate,
who after years of watching Steve testing drink recipes
heard a UB40 song and asked,
"Why are they only singing about Red Red Wine?
Don't they like cocktails?"

CONTENTS

INTRODUCTION

I'M DRINKING UP FOR LOST TIME. I was a good kid, a churchgoing kid who didn't have his first drink til the night of high school graduation. It was a sticky June evening, and I was at a party with the cool kids, playing Frisbee with a boy I hated, when I heard we were out of beer. I don't know why I thought Scott's parents would be amenable to making a beer run for a group of underaged kids on their lawn, but I figured it was worth a shot, and stumbled into their kitchen. Scott's mom, much to my satisfaction, turned out to be a model hostess. She dug deep into the back of her cabinet to find an oldish bottle of Manischewitz, which I finished on the lawn with that hateful Frisbee kid. I then went home and threw it all up on my own front lawn.

Even throughout college I remained a light drinker, although admittedly, it was the '80s and the popular cocktails just weren't for me. As a young bartender in stripes and "flair," I served my guests cotton candy–colored concoctions garnished with plastic animals and sugar rims in an effort to hide the flavor of the alcohol. The taste of spirits had long ago fallen out of style, and all sophistication was lost.

But years later, as a successful restaurateur in my own right, I found myself outside Audrey Saunders's Pegu Club on a cold Manhattan evening. I had heard that NYC was at the beginning of a cocktail resurgence, offering up well-crafted cocktails with a focus on quality ingredients and balance. Original recipes were being painstakingly researched and recreated, and I wanted to know more. So I pulled up a stool next to the hipsters and connoisseurs and ordered myself a gin Aviation. If there's any such thing as a gin epiphany, I had one.

Now, don't tell me you don't drink gin. I've heard it all before.

"No really, I can't drink gin…I'm terribly allergic."

I stand next to your table with my fearsome cocktail menu in hand. I'm really trying to talk you out of that cosmo. "You've had a bad experience with gin, right? Be honest."

You fess up. You had one of those nights in high school/one of those benders in college/one of those lost weekends in Vegas. You don't drink gin because it tastes too harsh or (even better) because it makes you "crazy". I cajole/strong-arm you into ordering a gin cocktail with the promise of paying for it if you don't like it…which you do. Of course you do. And I'm on to the next table.

Coming up through the ranks as I did, paired with my stint at Food Network, has made me a big believer in accessibility. As I cull these treasures for my own cocktail list, I consistently stress that we won't serve anything that guests couldn't make themselves. It feels pointless to introduce people to a sensational cocktail that can only be made with ingredients they can't get their hands on. Sharing unusable information is no fun to me.

One of the ways I demystify the movement is through the use of readily available ingredients in my cocktails; if something is not available locally, you will be able to find it for purchase online. And although there is a very exciting trend in lounges now of creating house bitters, making homemade tonics, and manufacturing ice, I won't require that of you either. You may choose to look into that at some point, but for now let's focus on inspiring and empowering you to pick up a cocktail shaker this weekend…or at 4:59 tonight; no judgment here.

I'm assuming you already see the glamour in playing the bartender, holding court as your guests watch you mix and muddle. And, of course, there is great satisfaction to be gained when the completed cocktail brings accolades. As Jerry Thomas, the father of modern mixology, put it, if you "fulfill their desires to their entire satisfaction [you] will not fail to acquire popularity and success." Let me repeat that:

you *"will not fail to acquire popularity and success."* Who doesn't want that? It's like a fantastic note stuffed inside one big bourbon-soaked fortune cookie.

The New Old Bar endeavors to fulfill your desire to, if not become a master bartender, have a go-to guide on the new craft cocktail scene. I have spent the years since my first stop at the Pegu Club researching vintage cocktail guides and testing hundreds of recipes. I've included two hundred of my favorites, most of them tried-and-true historical cocktails. You'll find the basic standards included among the outlandish and exotic, and many of my own original recipes as well as twists on the staples. I've also added recipes created by the talented mixologists at Hearty Restaurant. And in section four, you'll find Dan's recipes for easy to eat bar-top friendly snacks, along with his tips and musings.

For further "popularity and success" I urge you to commit some of the included back stories and toasts to memory. A drink that comes with a tale is infinitely more intoxicating, and one that starts with a toast is downright inspiring.

So, remembering that Julia Child credited her longevity to "red meat and gin," I want you to pick out a recipe and live the lush life.

On to the next table.

Steve McDonagh

A NOTE ON MODERATION

You'll note that many of these cocktails are "short pours," meaning they may be 3 to 6 ounces, and that's OK. These cocktails aren't meant to fill a fishbowl of a martini glass. The current cocktail movement is about savoring the potable, from the preparation, to the presentation, to the palate.

When properly made, the mixing glass yields a potion alive with the tiniest air bubbles, brightly scented with citrus zest, and served in a glass beaded with condensation. Harry Craddock, legendary head bartender of the American Bar at the London Savoy, understood this, which is why he said that the best way to enjoy a cocktail is "quickly; while it's laughing at you."

With that in mind, my end goal in writing *The New Old Bar* is to help you discover a buzz from the experience; not just from the alcohol. Because if you can show me a guy who can get to the bottom of a 10 ounce martini glass while the drink is still "laughing," I can show you a guy who is missing the point.

SPIRITS

AS WITH COOKING, USING THE FINEST INGREDIENTS IN YOUR COCKTAIL will yield the best results. This is why professional bartenders stock multiple brands of each spirit. Different brands produce different styles of a spirit, which in turn affects the balance of a cocktail. But for the home entertainer, the limitations of space and budget must be taken into account. I expect many of you will hope to purchase one bottle to suit all purposes, so with that in mind, I give you a short reference guide to help you choose wisely.

Primary

BRANDY is a distilled wine (from the Dutch *brandewijn* or "burnt wine") and is an absolute must for the modern cocktailer. Its uniquely warm and fruity flavor is the basis for many of our most beloved cocktails, including the Sidecar. At my own home bar I rely mainly on two types of brandy: an all-purpose VS Brandy for most drinks, and America's original distilled spirit, Applejack (Lairds being the consummate brand) for my apple cocktails. Other recipes may call for fruit brandies, such as apricot, kirschwasser (cherry brandy), or the fine French apple brandy Calvados. And every decent bar is equipped with a bottle of Peruvian pisco, the righteous South American grape brandy.

GIN is a light-bodied, clean, white spirit that is bonded with juniper and botanicals in one of two ways. It is either "compounded" which is evil and basically just adds juniper extracts and botanicals to the neutral spirit, or "distilled" which infuses the spirit with flavor through steeping or vapor and is delightful. Although juniper is generally the predominant flavor, it is the unique botanicals that give each gin its profile. For example, you'll find Hendrick's gin in Green Side (see page 81) because of its delicate infusion of rose petal and cucumber.

Gins are broken into the following categories:

✦ **LONDON DRY** is generally accepted to "play well" in mixed drinks. You'd be smart to ask your liquor store salesperson for an American distillery that makes a gin in the London Dry fashion. These "New American" gins are a mixologist's dream at the moment, with distilleries riffing on the classic recipe with amazing results.

✦ **PLYMOUTH GIN** is in its own category (it must be made in Plymouth, England) and is a bar staple for its excellent mixing qualities. It is bold, slightly fruity, and full bodied.

✦ **OLD TOM GIN** is a sweeter version of London Dry. The original gin called for in a Tom Collins, it is lightly sweetened and botanically intensive.

✦ **GENEVER** (Holland or Dutch gin) is referred to as the grandfather of what we now know as gin. It has two categories: the aromatic, almost white, whiskey-like old style ("oude") and the more neutral-flavored new ("jonge"). The jonge is comparable to London Dry Gin but is softer, with more subtle juniper.

RUM is a sweeter spirit due to its base in sugar cane or molasses. Aging and the casks used for aging define the characteristics of the rum. Some of the tiki drinks found in this book will call for three types of rum, and the results speak for themselves. Light (white or silver) rum is filtered after being aged in stainless steel and is the rum most frequently used in classic cocktails. Gold rum often has added caramel and is aged in oak casks, while heavily charred oak gives dark rum its rich, sweet characteristics. South American Demerara rum is an excellent dark rum, as is my personal favorite, Gosling's Black Seal. You will see recipes that specifically call for Gosling's in this book. Also in this category is Cachaca, a fine quality pure sugar cane rum from Brazil.

TEQUILA is made from blue agave plants. Label reading will tell you whether the tequila is 100 percent blue agave or tequila mixto (blended with cane syrups). The different categories (silver, gold, reposado, anejo, extra anejo) refer to how long the spirit has aged (or rested [reposado]). If you plan on buying one bottle for your bar, I recommend a reposado, as most cocktails in the craft movement call for this level. While mezcal is also made from the agave plant, it is a not a tequila. Its lush smoky qualities require a different preparation, and yes, mezcal is the one that sometimes has the worm.

VODKA is a clear distilled spirit with a base of barley, wheat, rye, or (less frequently) potatoes. Since vodka was not enjoyed by the general public until the 1950s, it largely missed out on the cocktail's renaissance. Although vodka can offer too strong a burn and too little flavor to find its way onto a classic cocktail list, I've included recipes that incorporate it for those who insist. When purchasing vodka, you should never consider anything other than a top-shelf brand with an eye to some of the wonderful newer organic options.

WHISKEY is the most complex of the spirits, with multiple nations producing versions in their own distinctive character from a mash of malted grains. At a minimum, your bar will need three types of whiskey: Scotch* (think smoky), bourbon (sweet), and rye (spicy/fruity). You will still find recipes requiring two additional types: Irish and blended. Choosing a brand for your bar is not as daunting as you may think. The craft cocktail movement has opened the floodgates to wonderful small batch brands that are surprisingly affordable. None of my included cocktails will call for something as expensive as a single-malt Scotch, for example.

*Any good Scot will tell you the correct spelling is Scotch whisky (without an 'e'). Let me put that out there, as I am a McDonagh, after all.

Secondary

ABSINTHE is a seductively bitter, astringent, anise-and-herb-tinged spirit. With a preparation that requires its own spoon and a communal fountain of cold water drip, it's certainly among the most high-maintenance spirits. Its unfair reputation as a cause of mania, epilepsy, and tuberculosis and its sordid association with Toulouse-Lautrec and a one-eared Van Gogh finally resulted in its infamous, nearly worldwide ban. Thankfully, the ban was lifted in 2007, and we can all enjoy "the green fairy."

ALLSPICE DRAM is also known as pimento dram and has a dark, spicy flavor that is essential to many tiki drinks. St. Elizabeth is my current brand of choice but others are available online. Some enterprising readers may choose to infuse their own; a quick Internet search will yield recipes and save you a bit of money.

AMARO is the term for a category of bitter Italian aperitifs. Amaros come in a range of brands, flavors, and intensities and work tremendously well in rounding out cocktails. Some of the amaros featured in *The New Old Bar* are Cynar, Amaro Averna, and Fernet Branca.

BENEDICTINE is a cognac-and-herb-based liqueur whose recipe is a highly guarded trade secret, ostensibly known to only three people at any given time. Its sweet and herbal warmth adds texture and spice to many vintage recipes. Paired with brandy, it is one of the Bs in B&B Liqueur.

CHARTREUSE has been made by monks in the Swiss Alps for over four hundred years from a recipe that includes 130 plants and herbs. While both are sweet and herbaceous, Green Chartreuse is more intensely spicy while Yellow Chartreuse has a more mellow, citrusy profile and carries a lower proof (80 versus 110).

CRÈME YVETTE is one of the success stories of a lost spirit being brought back to life by the cocktail resurgence. It is similar to crème de violette in that

that they are both floral and sweet, but they bring different levels of each of those characteristics to a cocktail. Crème cordials should not be confused with cream cordials. Unlike Baileys Irish Cream, they do not contain dairy; the crème title refers to the syrupy texture on the palate.

ELDERFLOWER LIQUEUR is a delicately flavored artisinal French liqueur distilled from elderflower blossoms. Its low sugar content and subtle floral notes really help it to play well with others. Do purchase a bottle for your liquor cabinet; it's wonderful added to sparkling wine or to a simple club soda highball.

GALLIANO is a thick, sweet herbal liqueur filled with the bold flavors of vanilla, star anise, and herbs. It is one of those types of very specific flavors that you can't replicate. I find it seductive and addicting and I love to pair it with orange.

LILLET is a French aperitif wine that comes in two varieties, Lillet Blanc and the sweeter and less frequently called for Lillet Rouge. It's lovely on the rocks with an orange slice and is vital for James Bond's signature Vesper (see page 139).

The original recipe for Lillet (formerly known as Kina Lillet) contained significantly more quinine and made for a more bitter cocktail addition. Cocchi Americano is the item on the market closest to that original product.

MARASCHINO LIQUEUR is my all-time favorite classic ingredient. Made from whole Marasca cherries (pit and all), maraschino adds a nutty fruitiness and velvety texture to cocktails. Buy Luxardo brand. You will find recipes that call for Cherry Heering as well, but aside from the cherry in their names, the two spirits have little in common. Cherry Heering is a dark, richly flavored brandy, and the two cannot be substituted.

ORANGE LIQUEUR will be the phrase used in this book to refer to triple sec and curaçao (Cointreau and Grand Marnier being brand names). Don't scrimp on this ingredient, as the cheaper ones can add too much alcohol burn or cloying sweetness to the cocktail.

SHERRY is a Spanish fortified wine that is finally enjoying a comeback. Its undeniable old-timey presence adds mystery to a cocktail. There are predominantly two types: fino (light and dry) and oloroso (sweet and rich). I tend to use sweet cream oloroso more frequently as it seems the most pleasing to the general palate, but dry fino is also included in the recipes.

VELVET FALERNUM is a subtly flavored liqueur with a sweet and spicy character of vanilla, almond, allspice, clove, and ginger. A quick Internet search will yield recipes if you're feeling adventurous, but that same search may just point out where to purchase it online.

VERMOUTH is a fortified wine. It comes in two forms with various names: Italian (or red or sweet) and French (or white or dry). Vermouth should be refrigerated. As a home bartender, you will go through your vermouth very slowly, so do not buy 750 mL bottles. Purchase half bottles that will fit in your fridge door, where they will last about six months.

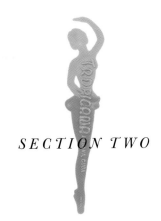

BASICS

Ingredients

PROHIBITION MAY HAVE LOST THE WAR AGAINST ALCOHOL, BUT IT BEAT the hell out of the cocktail. Aged liquor was in short supply after Prohibition. To combat this "drought," liquor companies realized they could stretch out the limited whiskey supply by blending it with non-aged, neutral grain spirits. Enter modern blended whiskey—light on flavor, easy to pair with club soda or juice in a rocks tumbler. Capitalizing on that success, marketers introduced a push for quickly produced, triple-distilled vodka. As Americans grew accustomed to this smooth and unflavored wallflower of a spirit, our palate began to shift. We lost our taste for the complex and richly flavored liquors that make up the well-balanced cocktail.

The decline continued with the jet age of the 1960s and the proliferation of "modern" pre-bottled cocktails. In the words of my Heublein's Club pamphlet, these ready-made concoctions make "home-made cocktails seem amateurish!" They also had the creepiest little barman mascot you've ever seen. Honestly, he'd put you off drinking altogether.

And the 1970s were no help, either. They added nails to the cocktail coffin in the form of imitation flavored sour mixes and concentrated juices sold in little plastic fruits. Adding insult to injury was a company that made freeze-dried cocktails in a pouch: "Sure Shot Instant Cocktails. Just add water!" In 1978, *Business Week* said "booze in a packet will soon be the Kool-Aid of the liquor industry." "Look at the advantages," the director of marketing told the *Milwaukee Journal*, "You could throw a couple of pouches in your fishing box!" A pouch of whiskey sours in my tackle box? You'd better believe I've been trying desperately to get my hands on one, and I don't even fish.

None of this is accepted in a pre-Prohibition cocktail. To return to my comparison with cooking, why is it that the ingredients in our glasses can be held to a lesser standard than those on our plates? Fresh and flavorful ingredients are key to the enjoyment of a proper libation.

JUICES

Use only fresh lemons and limes. Unless the cocktail recipe calls for sodium benzoate, sodium metabisulfite, or sodium sulfite (check those "real citrus juice" labels), there is no reason not to use an honest piece of citrus in your drink. If your fruit of choice is out of season, try to purchase a container of fresh squeezed. I do that most frequently with blood orange juice, as blood oranges can be difficult to find.

GARNISHES

Don't forget what we say about "eating with our eyes first." Garnishes dress up a naked cocktail and give the guest an idea of what's in store. But don't be fooled into thinking of them as mere decorations. The brine from olives and the essential oils of citrus twists are important flavoring agents.

✦ OLIVES

Does it sound geeky to say I love to shop for olives? There is a trove of thrilling jarred olives stuffed with everything from anchovy to jalapeños, and the accompanying brine makes for my favorite flavoring in Dirty Martinis. I recommend buying some fat Spanish green olives in brine. Keep in mind that you don't want to add oil-cured olives to a drink unless you're hoping for an oil slick to make its way across the surface of your martini.

One major caveat: jarred blue cheese olives are, as a rule and in a word, nasty. The blue cheese is usually gummy and has lost its tang by wallowing for an unknown time in the brine. The simple answer is to stuff your own. Use a toothpick to stuff a small rectangle of pungent blue cheese back into the empty cavity of a pitted olive. I've heard tell that these olives will keep for several weeks, but frankly, if you have any left over you've done it wrong.

✦ CHERRIES

I get it; every now and then that plump red balloon of a maraschino cherry adds a jaunty little party to your glass. And although I won't take issue with the occasional look for garnish's sake (or that bar trick where you tie the stem into a knot with your tongue, because that's just cool), they are filled with artificial dyes and packed in unnaturally flavored almond sugar syrup.

A much better way of preserving the cherries is with brandy, and making your own isn't as difficult as you may think. See page 150 for the recipe.

✦ HERBS

Keep herbs fresh and bright by laying them between layers of moist paper towel. At our bar we always leave bunches of fresh herbs in a bar glass with a little water, as you would with fresh cut flowers.

BITTERS

Bitters are a must-have for any well-stocked bar and are critical for making a well-balanced drink. Like seasoning on food, their warm, spicy, and herbal qualities transform a cocktail, adding complexity and depth.

Made by infusing alcohol with plant extracts, tree bark, fruit peels, and roots, bitters got their start in apothecary shops. It seems quaint, but there is scientific proof for their use as a homeopathic remedy. When our tongues meet bitter, our livers are stimulated to release bile. Bile aids in digestion. Score another for the Italians, whose age-old tradition is to take a bitter aperitif after a heavy meal.

But let's steer the conversation away from bile. Bitters are renowned by bartenders for another reason. Biting a soaked lemon wedge will absolutely, positively cure your hiccups. I am not a doctor. But I am a host, and as a host, I use bitters in another way. I like to offer my non-drinking guests a club soda with bitters and lime. The flavor is immensely more sophisticated than that of soft drinks and, when served in a wine glass, feels more "special occasion." With its next-to-nothing calorie count, this is also a great drink for dieters.

✦ ANGOSTURA AROMATIC BITTERS

Sort of the go-to bitters. Angostura is an aromatic, highly concentrated flavoring readily available in most grocery stores and easily identified by its oversized label. So vital is Angostura to the cocktail realm that a 2009 shortage led to hoarding and general panic behind the bars.

✦ PEYCHAUD'S

Nineteenth-century pharmacist Antoine Peychaud served his friends a cognac-based cocktail made with a dash of his own bitters. Peychaud's Bitters have a lightly sweet anise flavor and are mandatory for making his creation, the Sazerac.

✦ ORANGE BITTERS

An intense orange rind flavor makes these a personal favorite of mine. Orange bitters are a style of bitters, and a few brands are available, most notably from Fee Brothers and cocktail great Gary Regan.

✦ OTHER FLAVORS

One of the more exciting by-products of the cocktail renaissance is a resurgence in bitters formulations. Not only are products such as peach, lavender, grapefruit, and rhubarb becoming available on shelves and online, but bartenders have taken to making their own. Even though making house-made bitters is really quite a simple process of infusing grain alcohol, I promise I haven't included any recipes that force you to mix your own batch…but you might want to try it for fun. If you'd like to play with bitters (the spice rack of your bar) a good place to start is online with The Bitter Truth (the-bitter-truth.com).

SIMPLE SYRUP

Simple syrup is the best way to ensure total incorporation of sugar to a cocktail. The recipe is a 1:1 ratio of white sugar and water, boiled until the sugar is completely dissolved. The recipes in *The New Old Bar* call for both simple syrup and turbinado syrup. Turbinado syrup is exactly the same ratio, but it is made with raw sugar. Raw (or unbleached) sugar has a richer, darker flavor and is better suited to cocktails containing brown spirits.

EGGS

How do I explain this without setting off your *News at 5* alarms? Raw eggs were used with great frequency in classic cocktails. A shaken egg white emulsifies and binds the components, adding a luxurious silky mouthfeel that can't be recreated. The cocktail revivalists are back to using raw eggs in cocktails, and while I don't want to underplay the hazards of salmonella, with proper steps you should feel comfortable serving egg drinks as well. Here are some tips:

- ✦ Buy them fresh, keep them cold, and use them quick.

- ✦ Rinse the outer shell before use, and don't let the egg white come in contact with the outer shell.

- ✦ Adding alcohol and fresh citrus to egg whites helps kill bacteria…oh… lucky you!

- ✦ If you're concerned, buy eggs that are pasteurized in the shell. They won't get as fluffy, but they're deemed raw-food safe.

ICE

Look to Tokyo if you really want to feel like an underachieving slacker. To no one is the act of chilling a drink a greater art form than to the members of the NBA (Nippon Bartending Association).

✦ CLARITY FOR THE SLACKER

Ice is a vital ingredient of your cocktail. Once again, as with cooking, we want to use the freshest ingredients available (especially with something as inexpensive as frozen water). How long have the cubes sat in your freezer absorbing odors? Empty your ice trays and your freezer's ice bin the day before the party to ensure that you'll have clean ice on hand. You can also eliminate impurities by using filtered water in your ice trays.

✦ CLARITY FOR THE JAPANESE

Members of the Nippon Bartending Association slowly freeze their ice blocks over two or three days. The ice freezes from the outer edges, causing the air bubbles to move toward the center. Once fully formed, the center section is removed, leaving a crystal clear, super dense block that melts more slowly.

✦ SIZE AND SHAPE FOR THE SLACKER

For the cocktail geek, ice size is a key factor. It's all about surface area—the larger the cube, the less it melts and the less water is incorporated into the cocktail. With the obvious exceptions of cocktails that call for crushed ice, steer clear of hollow ice, ice that has begun to melt, and the slivers in the ice tray.

✦ SIZE AND SHAPE FOR THE JAPANESE

Ice is so important in Japanese bar culture that top bartenders rinse each individual cube in mineral water to soften the edges. Why? Because rough edges will cause sparkling additions to lose their effervescence more rapidly.

✦ LARGE CHUNKS FOR THE SLACKER

We serve cocktails such as an Old Fashioned with one large chunk of ice; again, this creates less surface area and less dilution. To do this at home, simply fill a shallow pan with water and place it in the freezer. Once it has frozen, run warm water around the outside of the pan to remove the ice. Place it on a non-skid surface and use a clean ice pick or (be careful!) a sharp kitchen knife to break off a chunk that fits your glass.

✦ LARGE CHUNKS FOR THE JAPANESE

A Japanese bartender will take four minutes to personally hand carve a perfectly smooth sphere from a large chunk of ice for your cocktail. He isn't satisfied until it will roll freely around your glass like a marble. You slacker.

Tools

FACT ONE: THE ADULT BEVERAGE MARKET IS BIG MONEY AND IS TRENDING super hot. Fact Two: You can't make a proper cocktail without the proper tools. Fact Three: Facts One and Two result in a glut of poorly made, unnecessary tools demanding your attention on the shelves. Do yourself a favor and save the money on the dust-gathering accessory carousel with the shiny hanging gee-gaws and just buy the tools you need. If you buy quality tools with substance and weight and assemble them before your party starts, you "will not fail to acquire popularity and success"!

SHAKER

There are two types of shakers, the cobbler and the Boston shaker. They both do the same thing, and your choice is a matter of personal preference.

✦ COBBLER SHAKER

This is the type I use at home and the easiest for the novice bartender. It is most frequently a tempered steel shaker with a tight-fitting lid that has a built-in strainer and cap. The shaker is arguably your most important bar tool and the seal is its most important attribute, so do not buy one because it is cheap or, even worse, because it is pretty!

✦ BOSTON SHAKER

This is what you see bartenders using professionally. It consists of a heavy mixing glass and a flat-bottomed tin shaker. When put together, the two pieces form an airtight seal for shaking. To break the seal, you smack the palm of your hand against the upside-down glass. The clear mixing glass is excellent for stirring drinks and being able to see what you're pouring. However, the Boston shaker requires practice and confidence to use properly.

STRAINER

If you are using a Boston shaker you will always need a Hawthorne strainer. It's a flat sieve with a spring around the edges that hugs the glass. Be sure to buy one that fits your mixing glass. Thicker recipes with muddled fruits (see Grapefruit Smash, page 80) are best strained through a Hawthorne strainer as the holes on the cobbler shaker will clog.

MUDDLER

My vote for the coolest bar tool; a wooden or stainless bat of sorts used to crush fruits and herbs. When purchasing a muddler, keep length in mind. It should be 8 to 10 inches to protect your knuckles from smacking against the glass. The material is personal preference, but if you are like me and prefer old-school wood, be sure to avoid lacquered coatings as you don't want lacquer to chip away into your cocktails. When you're in a pinch, a wooden spoon will do as a muddler.

JIGGER

Today's cocktail recipes are dependent on exact amounts for balance, which has made free pouring a thing of the past. It used to be necessary to have two separate double-cup jiggers to meet all the measurement requirements, but no longer. You can meet all those needs with one double jigger that has ⅓ increments on one side and ¼ increments on the other. OXO is my brand of choice right now. It is easy to read and has a rubber grip.

OTHER NEEDS

✦ **BAR KNIFE AND SMALL CUTTING BOARD**

✦ **ICE BUCKET AND ICE SCOOP**

Never use a glass as a scoop; clear glass chips are undetectable in ice and pose a major health hazard. Never use ice tongs for that matter, either, because they're just so annoying.

✦ **CITRUS SQUEEZER**

Wonderful vise-grip citrus squeezers are widely available now. They are simple to use and easy to clean and have a strainer to catch the seeds. A great bar investment; I haven't used a reamer or a bowl juicer since.

✦ CORKSCREW

I am a fan of the traditional waiter's corkscrew that has the foil blade, worm, and bottle rest that fits on the lip for leverage. Choose a heavy one.

✦ BOTTLE OPENER OR "CHURCH KEY"

✦ LONG-HANDLED BAR SPOON

Aside from stirring drinks like Manhattans, the twisted handle serves a specific purpose in stirring drinks with crushed ice. Plunge the bar spoon into your finished cocktail and, taking the handle between your thumb and forefinger, twirl it back and forth as you slowly draw the spoon up and down through the cocktail. The bar spoon is also very useful for floating spirits over the top of tiki drinks and for measuring out very small amounts, as is often necessary with absinthe.

✦ NUTMEG GRATER

✦ CANVAS ICE BAG (LEWIS BAG) or lint-free towel for making crushed ice

✦ PICKS OR SKEWERS for olives and similar garnishes

✦ STRAWS

✦ BAR TOWEL

I can't get through a party without two: one as a working base to rest my wet equipment and one thrown over my shoulder like some Mick bartender from a Bowery Boys episode.

✦ BEVERAGE NAPKINS

Because you might have forgotten if I didn't put it on your list.

✦ TRASH CAN

Because you absolutely would have forgotten if I didn't put it on your list.

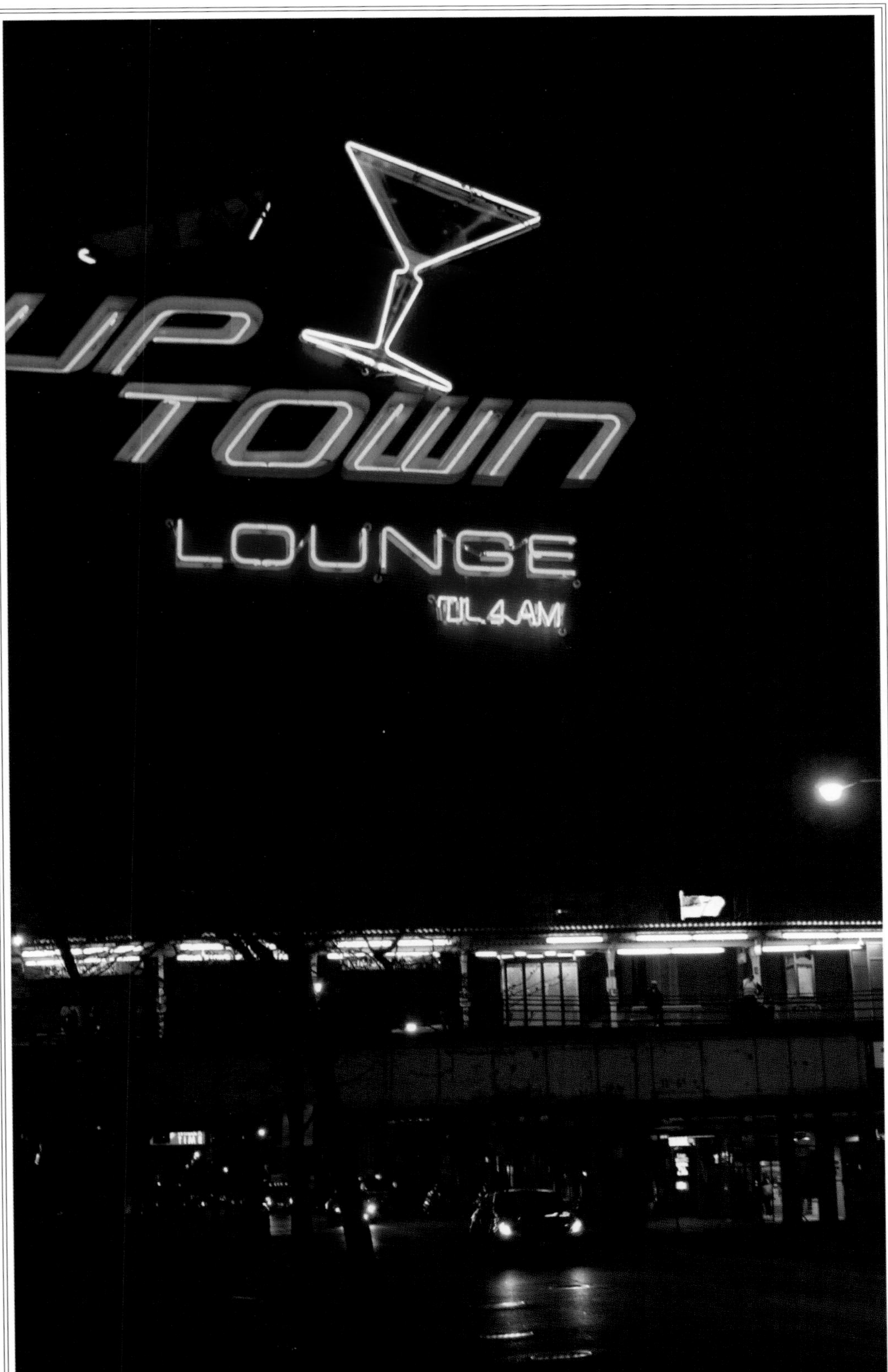
UP
TOWN
LOUNGE
TIL 4 AM

Techniques

POSSIBLY THE MOST GLARING DIFFERENCE I SEE WITH THE NEW OLD BAR
is its aesthetic. When I first started tending bar, we would practice for hours tossing
bottles over our shoulders and behind our backs. We'd free pour two bottles in each
hand, the liquor flowing high above the shakers. I would shout drink orders back to
one customer while taking money from another and kicking the cooler doors shut
with my foot (that is, when my foot wasn't on fire; I was often the victim of a rather
frightening prank involving Bacardi 151 and a match).

But now we're looking backwards to a more sophisticated cocktail experience, and
the establishments and the bartenders reflect the new aesthetic. Five years ago you'd
be hard-pressed to keep it together if you were greeted by a bartender with a waxed
handlebar mustache, but now his vest, arm garter, and slicked hair speak of experience,
knowledge, and juniper history. Tom Cruise and his neon bar be damned, this is much
cooler.

SHAKE

We've all heard people who think they're hilarious put on a Sean Connery voice and
say, "Shaken, not stirred." So let's discuss why we sometimes choose one over the
other…and, while we're at it, let's you and I make a pact that we won't do that Sean
Connery thing anymore.

I'll admit that I'm a shaker. I like the ritual of slapping a mixing glass together and
listening to the ice rattle over my right shoulder. But even though it's hard for me,
there are times when all I really need to do is stir. The basic rule of thumb is to stir
drinks that contain only spirits and to shake drinks that have added juices, sweeteners,
and cream.

Aside from the obvious chilling factor, there are two main benefits to shaking a cocktail
with ice. The first benefit is that the harsh edges of the alcohol are softened through
the addition of diluted ice water. In fact, diluted water accounts for as much as 25
percent of a mixed drink.

The second benefit comes from adding aeration. The tiny air bubbles created by shaking add life and texture to a drink. While this is perfect for a citrus-heavy standard like the daiquiri, a martini is the opposite. A spirits-only cocktail should feel weighty and silky on the tongue, without the effervescence.

The shaking technique varies, and you'll find your own comfort zone as you practice. Add ingredients to a shaker filled about two-thirds with ice before shaking vigorously for ten to fifteen seconds. There's an old bartender's chestnut that you should put into practice: "You're trying to wake the drink up, not send it to sleep". Be sure to face the open end of the shaker away from your guests as you shake; you don't want droplets or spillage tossed in their direction. You'll know that you've successfully created a crisp cocktail when frost appears on the outside of the shaker.

If you feel like you need more help, there are some wonderful videos on YouTube that will help the visual learners. I'm a fan of Jeffrey Morgenthaler; I think he's a good teacher.

DRY SHAKE

This is the method used for frothing egg whites in a cocktail. Shaking the egg in an empty mixing glass breaks down the proteins and emulsifies the egg, allowing the other ingredients to better blend. The first step is to shake the egg vigorously (for…I don't know…how long is "shake the hell out of it"?) before adding spirits, juices, and ice and shaking again. When done properly, this will result in a thick, frothy head and an unbeatably silky cocktail.

If you aren't achieving the heady results you hoped for, try removing the spring off a Hawthorne strainer (very simple to do) and including that in the shaker to act as an agitator.

MUDDLE

Muddling is a method of extracting juice and oils directly into your cocktail and is essential for drinks such as juleps and mojitos.

There are a few things to keep in mind, the first being safety. Always muddle in a thick mixing glass or stainless bar tin to avoid accidental breakage. The second is that you should muddle herbs less aggressively than fruits, as you don't want to pulverize the delicate leaves. You're only trying to release the essential oils, and you don't want to be left with dark, bruised, and limp leaves languishing in your glass.

When I muddle, I always start by adding a little of the simple syrup or other liquor called for in the recipe. Steady the mixing glass on the bar or tabletop with one hand while repeatedly mashing the muddler down onto the fruit with the other. Give your wrist a quarter-turn twist as you smash down, as the most effective part of muddling is the follow-through.

Lastly, muddling items such as peeled ginger or large fruits may leave undesirable bits and require double straining (see Kochi Cobbler, page 90). To do this, simply strain the contents of the cocktail shaker through a second strainer held above the glass. I use a small-handled tea strainer.

BAR FRUIT

✦ TWIST

To really appreciate the twist, you should taste a cocktail before and after its addition. So much more than color, the twist adds both flavor and aroma. We shouldn't neglect the sexiness the citrus scents bring to the glass.

Cut a strip about 1½ by 1 inch with a paring knife or sharp wide vegetable peeler. Keep a little of the white pith for sturdiness, but not so much that you add its bitterness to your drink. Twist, pinch, or squeeze the peel over the cocktail's surface and then run it around the perimeter of the glass before dropping it in.

Put your own twist on twists by experimenting with length and curliness. Some people use channel knives with great effect. Sadly, I am not one of those people.

✦ WEDGE

A lime or lemon wedge is best used when a little extra juice may be required. A finished wedge can be squeezed into the drink at the last minute and dropped into the cocktail or, if slotted, can rest on the lip of the glass for presentation and the guest's option. You should be able to get about six wedges out of a lime and about eight from a lemon. Be sure to pick out any stray lemon seeds that are poking out before you use the wedge as garnish.

✦ WHEEL

Fairly self explanatory, a wheel is a lemon or lime round cut vertically through the 'equator' of the fruit. These are used on the edge of the glass for dramatic garnish or floated on the surface of a drink. Be sure to cut a slit through the peel of the fruit to the center to allow for the glass rim.

✦ FLAG

A flag refers to a maraschino cherry speared onto a fruit slice. An orange flag is a half-moon orange slice and a maraschino held together with a toothpick, a pineapple flag is a cherry-skewered pineapple wedge, and so on. At our bar we prefer to use a long skewer to spear a brandied cherry in a blanket of orange peel.

Thrust the skewer through one side of a widely cut orange peel, then through a brandied cherry and back through the orange on the other side, so that the orange peel is wrapped around the cherry.

FLAME

I'm sure "Cocktail King" Dale DeGroff is not the first person to flame the oils of citrus rind, but it seems he now owns this procedure and I can't ever flame a zest without him coming to mind. Hold a 1-inch round of peel (skin side facing the drink) between thumb and forefinger, being careful not to squeeze and dispel the oils. In the other hand, hold a lit match or, my preference, a long matchstick lighter, between the peel and the cocktail. As you squeeze the peel over the surface of the cocktail, the oils will spark through the flame and leave a lovely, caramelized, aromatic finish to the drink. You can then toss in the garnish as you normally would.

RIM

Run a lemon or lime wedge around the perimeter of the glass to moisten. Meanwhile, prepare a shallow plate with the rimming spice, sugar, or salt. Place the glass upside-down onto the plate so that the dry ingredients stick to the outside of the rim. Now here's the tricky part: it should only cling to the *outside* of the rim. You don't want excess seasoning to fall into your cocktail and ruin the balance. Here's the other tricky part: be light handed; the rimming spice is a garnish and it should be subtle. Nothing ruins a sunny day quicker than having to chew through a wall of rock salt to get to your margarita.

RINSE

Coating the inside of the glass with flavor will keep assertive spirits from overpowering a drink. Pour a splash of liquor into the chilled glass. Swirl it around to coat the sides and up toward the inner rim. Empty the glass of excess.

CHILL

I can't decide what I love more about my 1960s *Fleischmann's Mixer's Manual*. It's a toss-up between the retro pop graphics and the compelling insights, such as "Some guests pre-cool both liquor and glassware. It's a good practice."

Either way, there's no need to argue with Fleischmann. The easiest way to do this is by filling your coupe with ice and a little water *before* you make the drink. Ideally, by the time you're ready to present the cocktail, there will be beads of condensation on the outside of the glass. Dump the ice out and serve your drink in the freshly chilled glass. I have heard people suggest leaving stemware in the freezer, but I don't know a lot of folks who have the space for that. Do that if you can, but be wary of breakage.

STOCK

The caterer in me cannot let this chapter proceed without reminding you of what others will forget: how much ice you will need. Using fresh ice for each cocktail (and you must) really adds up. When having a party, the rule of thumb is 2 pounds per guest, which will include enough ice for you to chill your beer and wine in a cooler you can place near your bar.

PAY STATION
LONG DISTANCE TELEPHONE
1) HAVE NICKEL READY;
2) LISTEN FOR DIAL TONE;
3) DIAL NUMBER DESIRED;
4) QUICKLY DEPOSIT NICKEL IN NICKEL SLOT WHEN PARTY ANSWERS.
COIN RETURN

COCKTAILS

AFFINITY

- 1 OUNCE (30 mL) SCOTCH WHISKY
- 1 OUNCE (30 mL) DRY VERMOUTH
- 1 OUNCE (30 mL) SWEET VERMOUTH
- 2 DASHES ORANGE BITTERS
- LEMON TWIST (FOR GARNISH)

Combine the ingredients in a cocktail shaker filled with ice. Stir well. Strain into a chilled coupe and serve garnished with a lemon twist.

YIELD: 1 COCKTAIL

AIRMAIL

- ¾ OUNCE (23 mL) LIGHT RUM
- 1½ OUNCES (45 mL) HONEY LIQUEUR
- ½ OUNCE (15 mL) FRESH LEMON JUICE
- SPARKLING WINE OR PROSECCO
- LEMON TWIST (FOR GARNISH)

Combine the rum, honey liqueur, and lemon juice in a cocktail shaker filled with ice. Shake well. Strain into a chilled coupe and top with sparkling wine. Serve garnished with a lemon twist.

YIELD: 1 COCKTAIL

ALASKA COCKTAIL

This drink has nothing at all to do with Alaska. However, the vibrant combination of gin and 80 proof chartreuse can certainly help you to see Russia from your barstool.

> 2 OUNCES (60 ML) GIN
> ¾ OUNCE (23 ML) YELLOW CHARTREUSE
> DASH ORANGE BITTERS
> LEMON TWIST (FOR GARNISH)

Combine the ingredients in a cocktail shaker filled with ice. Stir well. Strain into a chilled coupe and serve garnished with a lemon twist.

> *YIELD: 1 COCKTAIL*

ALBINO GRASSHOPPER ➤

> 1½ OUNCES (45 ML) LIGHT RUM
> ½ OUNCE (15 ML) WHITE CRÈME DE CACAO
> 1 OUNCE (30 ML) HALF-AND-HALF
> ½ OUNCE (15 ML) MINT SYRUP (SEE ROSEMARY SYRUP, PAGE 148)
> ¼ TEASPOON BENEDICTINE
> FRESH MINT (FOR GARNISH)

Combine the ingredients in a cocktail shaker filled with ice. Shake very well. Strain into a chilled coupe and serve garnished with fresh mint.

> *YIELD: 1 COCKTAIL*

ALGONQUIN

Named for the hotel where Dorothy Parker allegedly said, "I'd rather have a bottle in front of me than a frontal lobotomy." And even though the members of the Algonquin Round Table probably drank martinis, you might want to make up a batch of these and see if you feel witty.

> 1½ OUNCES (45 ML) RYE
> ¾ OUNCE (23 ML) DRY VERMOUTH
> ¾ OUNCE (23 ML) FRESH PINEAPPLE JUICE
> ORANGE PEEL (FOR GARNISH)

Combine the ingredients in a cocktail shaker filled with ice. Shake well. Strain into a chilled coupe and serve garnished with an orange peel twist.

> *YIELD: 1 COCKTAIL*

◄ AMERICANO

1½ ounces (45 mL) Campari

1½ ounce (45 mL) sweet vermouth

3-4 ounces (90-120 mL) club soda

Orange slice (for garnish)

Combine the Campari and vermouth in a double rocks glass filled with ice.
Top with club soda. Serve garnished with an orange slice.

YIELD: 1 COCKTAIL

ANGEL'S TIT

Maraschino cherry

1½ ounces (45 mL) maraschino liqueur

¾ ounce (23 mL) half-and-half or heavy cream

Drop the maraschino cherry into a sherry glass. Pour the maraschino liqueur into the
glass and create a layered effect by gently pouring the cream over the back side
of a spoon into the glass. It should float on the top of the maraschino liqueur.

YIELD: 1 COCKTAIL

APPLECART

*This is an apple brandy sidecar which some call an "Apple Car". This makes no sense—
there's no such thing as an apple car. I'm starting a movement to call it the much more
sensible "Applecart." Join me. I'm published.*

1½ ounces (45 mL) applejack

¾ ounce (23 mL) orange liqueur

½ ounce (15 mL) fresh lemon juice

Lemon twist (for garnish)

Combine the ingredients in a cocktail shaker filled with ice. Shake well. Strain into a
chilled coupe and serve garnished with a lemon twist.

YIELD: 1 COCKTAIL

ARTICHOKE SOUR ⟁

> 1 EGG WHITE
>
> 2 OUNCES (60 mL) CYNAR LIQUEUR
>
> 1 OUNCE (30 mL) SIMPLE SYRUP
>
> ½ OUNCE (15 mL) FRESH LEMON JUICE
>
> BRANDIED CHERRY FLAG (FOR GARNISH)

Dry shake the egg white (see page 35). Add the remaining ingredients and ice to the cocktail shaker and shake vigorously a second time. Strain into a double old fashioned glass filled with ice. Serve garnished with a brandied cherry flag.

> *YIELD: 1 COCKTAIL*

AVIATION COCKTAIL

This is the cocktail I most frequently recommend for the non-gin drinkers. It's a perfect example of how gin is more than just an alcoholic ingredient, and how it adds flavor and depth to a cocktail. The Aviation is silky, crisp, and slightly fruity. Some will tell you that an Aviation must include crème de violette. For that, see its sister drink, the Blue Moon (page 55).

2 OUNCES (60 mL) GIN

1 OUNCE (30 mL) MARASCHINO LIQUEUR

½ OUNCE (15 mL) FRESH LEMON JUICE

BRANDIED CHERRY (FOR GARNISH)

Combine the ingredients in a cocktail shaker filled with ice. Shake well. Strain into a chilled coupe and serve garnished with a brandied cherry.

YIELD: 1 COCKTAIL

BACARDI COCKTAIL

Want a good marketing story? In 1936, as a "matter of honor, pride, and survival," Bacardi took bar owners to the New York Supreme Court, winning a suit that ensured that no other rum could be used in making this, their namesake cocktail.

2 OUNCES (60 mL) BACARDI LIGHT RUM

1 OUNCE (30 mL) FRESH LIME JUICE

¼ OUNCE (8 mL) GRENADINE (SEE PAGE 146)

Combine the ingredients in a cocktail shaker filled with ice. Shake well. Strain into a chilled coupe and serve ungarnished.

YIELD: 1 COCKTAIL

BACON CINNAMON SANGAREE

*The Sangaree derives from the same root word as sangria (*sangre, *meaning "blood") and dates back to the 1700s. They always call for fresh nutmeg and, most frequently, for the addition of port. In this case I opted against port and chose the most obvious substitute…which is, of course, bacon.*

2 OUNCES BACON-INFUSED BOURBON (SEE PAGE 144)

1 OUNCE (30 mL) APPLEJACK

½ OUNCE (15 mL) CINNAMON SYRUP (SEE PAGE 146)

1 WHOLE NUTMEG

FRESH SAGE (FOR GARNISH)

Combine the bourbon, applejack and cinnamon syrup in a cocktail shaker filled with ice. Shake well. Strain into a double rocks glass with one large ice chunk. Top the cocktail with a dusting of freshly ground nutmeg. Release the essential oils and aroma of the sage by holding it in your palm and clapping your hands together. Serve garnished with the sage leaf across the ice.

YIELD: 1 COCKTAIL

BAMBOO

1½ OUNCES (45 mL) FINO SHERRY

1½ OUNCES (45 mL) DRY VERMOUTH

2 DASHES ORANGE BITTERS

DASH ANGOSTURA AROMATIC BITTERS

LEMON TWIST (FOR GARNISH)

Combine the ingredients in a cocktail shaker filled with ice. Stir well. Strain into a chilled coupe and serve garnished with a lemon twist.

YIELD: 1 COCKTAIL

BASIL BUCK

3 OR 4 LARGE FRESH BASIL LEAVES (PLUS MORE FOR GARNISH)

2 OUNCES (60 mL) GIN (HENDRICK'S RECOMMENDED)

½ OUNCE (15 mL) GINGER SYRUP (SEE PAGE 146)

½ OUNCE (15 mL) FRESH LEMON JUICE

GINGER BEER

Muddle the basil leaves in a tall collins glass. Combine the gin, ginger syrup, and lemon juice in a cocktail shaker filled with ice. Shake well. Pour the entire contents of the shaker into the collins glass over the muddled basil and add more ice if needed. Top with ginger beer, and serve garnished with fresh basil.

YIELD: 1 COCKTAIL

BASIL JULEP

2 FRESH BASIL LEAVES (PLUS MORE FOR GARNISH)

¼ OUNCE (8 mL) FRESH LIME JUICE

2 OUNCES (60 mL) BOURBON

1½ OUNCES (45 mL) VELVET FALERNUM

In a sturdy glass or cocktail shaker, muddle the basil leaves and the lime juice. Add the bourbon, the falernum, and ice and shake well. Strain into a double old fashioned glass with ice. Serve garnished with a sprig of basil.

YIELD: 1 COCKTAIL

BEE'S KNEES ⋀

GRANULATED SUGAR*

2 OUNCES (60 ML) GIN

¾ OUNCE (23 ML) LAVENDER SYRUP (SEE PAGE 148)

½ OUNCE (15 ML) FRESH LEMON JUICE

FRESH LAVENDER (FOR GARNISH)

Rim a chilled coupe with sugar and set aside. Combine the gin, lavender syrup, and lemon juice in a cocktail shaker filled with ice. Shake well. Strain into the sugar-rimmed coupe and serve garnished with fresh lavender.

Dried lavender can be added to the granulated sugar for garnish.

YIELD: 1 COCKTAIL

BERMUDIAN ROSE

One of "a selection of the most suitable cocktails" from Café Royal Cocktail Book, *1937.*

1¼ OUNCES (38 ML) GIN

¾ OUNCE (23 ML) APRICOT BRANDY

½ OUNCE (15 ML) FRESH LEMON JUICE

¼ OUNCE (8 ML) GRENADINE (SEE PAGE 146)

2 DASHES ORANGE BITTERS

LEMON WHEEL (FOR GARNISH)

Combine the ingredients in a cocktail shaker filled with ice. Shake well. Strain into a chilled coupe and serve garnished with a lemon wheel.

YIELD: 1 COCKTAIL

BERTHA

This is most probably named after Doña Bertha, proprietor of a popular bar in Taxco, Mexico in the 1930s. Her name also comes up as one of the many possible inventors of the margarita.

1¾ OUNCES (53 ML) TEQUILA REPOSADO

½ OUNCE (15 ML) FRESH GRAPEFRUIT JUICE

½ OUNCE (15 ML) FRESH LIME JUICE

½ OUNCE (15 ML) GRENADINE (SEE PAGE 146)

GRAPEFRUIT PEEL (FOR GARNISH)

Combine the ingredients in a cocktail shaker filled with ice. Shake well. Strain into a double rocks glass filled with ice. Serve garnished with a grapefruit peel twist.

YIELD: 1 COCKTAIL

BETWEEN THE SHEETS

1½ OUNCE (45 ML) APPLEJACK

½ OUNCE (15 ML) BENEDICTINE

½ OUNCE (15 ML) ORANGE LIQUEUR

¾ OUNCE (23 ML) FRESH LEMON JUICE

ORANGE PEEL (FOR GARNISH)

Combine the ingredients in a cocktail shaker filled with ice. Shake well. Strain into a chilled coupe and serve garnished with a flamed orange peel.

YIELD: 1 COCKTAIL

BIJOU

1½ ounces (45 mL) gin

1 ounce (30 mL) Green Chartreuse

1 ounce (30 mL) dry vermouth

Brandied cherry (for garnish)

Combine the ingredients in a cocktail shaker filled with ice. Stir well. Strain into a chilled coupe and serve garnished with a brandied cherry.

YIELD: 1 COCKTAIL

BISON GRASS CRUSTA

I am torn about telling you how to properly garnish this drink, as I don't want to scare you away from it. The Crusta is a very old "fancy cocktail" whose name refers to the sugared lemon peel that forms a crust around the inside rim of the glass. The rind sticks up above the glass so that with the proper sugar seal the lemon becomes an extension of the glass, and you actually drink from the rind. The pineapple syrup used in my version negates the need for a sugar rim, but to stay true to the cocktail's spirit you should go overboard with your lemon garnish. Use a spiral of half a lemon to get the right effect, and either line the inside of the glass with it or leave a large portion hanging festively from the rim.

2 ounces (60 mL) Bison Grass Vodka*

1 ounce (30 mL) fresh lemon juice

1 ounce (30 mL) pineapple syrup (see page 148)

Lemon peel (for garnish)

Combine the ingredients in a cocktail shaker filled with ice. Shake well. Strain into a chilled coupe, and serve garnished with a lemon peel (see description).

* Bison Grass Vodka is a dry Polish vodka that owes its distinctive herbal flavor to buffalo grass. Also known as Żubrówka, it has been mass produced since before prohibition.

YIELD: 1 COCKTAIL

BLACK RUSSIAN*

1 ½ ounce (45 mL) vodka

¾ ounce (23 mL) coffee liqueur

Combine the vodka and coffee liqueur in a highball glass filled with ice. Stir and serve ungarnished.

To make a White Russian, just add ½ ounce (15 mL) cream before stirring.

YIELD: 1 COCKTAIL

BLOOD AND SAND

What a treat this cocktail is. Tart, sweet, juicy, strong. Substituting regular orange juice for the blood orange will result in a waste of ingredients. Wait until you can find them fresh (in winter) or search out a freshly squeezed bottled brand.

2 ounces (60 mL) Scotch whisky

1 ounce (30 mL) blood orange juice

1 ounce (30 mL) Lillet Rouge

1 ounce (30 mL) maraschino liqueur

Brandied cherry flag (for garnish)

Combine the ingredients in a cocktail shaker filled with ice. Shake well. Strain into a chilled coupe and serve garnished with a brandied cherry flag.

YIELD: 1 COCKTAIL

BLOODY BULL

2 ounces (60 mL) vodka

2 ounces (60 mL) tomato juice

2 ounces (60 mL) beef broth, chilled

½ teaspoon prepared horseradish

Tabasco to taste

Salt to taste

Beef jerky (for garnish)

Combine the vodka, tomato juice, beef broth, and horseradish in a cocktail shaker filled with ice. Pour the contents of the shaker into a second mixing glass and repeat back and forth until chilled. Add Tabasco and salt to taste. Stir and serve garnished with a stick of beef jerky.

YIELD: 1 COCKTAIL

BLOODY MARY MIX

The quintessential brunch cocktail. People are finicky and opinionated about their Bloody Marys. I put this drink in the same category as chicken wings, in that folks who tolerate heat enjoy challenging their taste buds by making it as hot as they can stand. I advise against this. 'Heat' is not a flavor; in fact, it dulls the taste buds and leaves you with nothing to savor other than the heat itself.

This blend not only has the required spicy kick but intriguing layers of flavor. The dark malt vinegar tang and the chewy sweetness of the tamarind will have your guests asking about the recipe.

2 CUPS (474 mL) TOMATO JUICE

2 CUPS (474 mL) VEGETABLE JUICE (V-8)

2 TABLESPOONS MALT VINEGAR

2 TEASPOONS MOLASSES

2 TEASPOONS TAMARIND PASTE*

1 TEASPOON PREPARED HORSERADISH

1 TEASPOON ANCHOVY PASTE

1 TEASPOON SALT

1½ TEASPOONS CELERY SALT

1½ TEASPOONS CAYENNE

½ TEASPOON CHILI POWDER

Combine the ingredients in a 1-quart pitcher and stir. Serve immediately, or refrigerate overnight if possible. For the Bloody Mary Cocktail, pour 1½ ounces (45 mL) vodka into a tall glass filled with ice, top with the Bloody Mary Mix (about 6–8 ounces [180–240 mL]), and stir. Serve garnished with flair and creativity.

*Tamarind paste can be found in specialty supermarkets, Asian markets, and Indian markets.

YIELD: APPROXIMATELY 1 QUART

BLUE BLAZER

Arguably the drink that Jerry Thomas was best known for, the Blue Blazer is basically a flaming arc of Scotch tossed between silver-plated mugs. I do not expect you to make this drink. I do not recommend that you attempt to make this drink. But any historic recipe whose instructions all but warn "drop and roll" simply must be included.

2 OUNCES (60 ML) SCOTCH WHISKY

1½ OUNCES (45 ML) BOILING WATER

2 TEASPOONS SUGAR

In Jerry's words: "Put the whiskey and the boiling water [and sugar] in one mug, ignite the liquid with fire, and while blazing, mix both ingredients by pouring them four or five times from one mug to the other…the novice…should be careful not to scald himself…[and] it will be necessary to practice for some time with cold water."

YIELD: 1 COCKTAIL

BLUE MOON

2 OUNCES (60 ML) GIN

½ OUNCE (15 ML) CRÈME DE VIOLETTE

½ OUNCE (15 ML) FRESH LEMON JUICE

LEMON PEEL (FOR GARNISH)

Combine the ingredients in a cocktail shaker filled with ice. Shake well. Strain into a chilled coupe, and serve garnished with a flamed lemon peel.

YIELD: 1 COCKTAIL

BLUEBERRY SMASH

12–14 BLUEBERRIES (PLUS MORE FOR GARNISH)

1 SPRIG ROSEMARY

½ OUNCE (15 ML) SIMPLE SYRUP

1½ OUNCES (45 ML) VS BRANDY

1 OUNCE (30 ML) CRÈME DE VIOLETTE

¼ OUNCE (8 ML) FRESH LEMON JUICE

In a sturdy glass or cocktail shaker, lightly muddle the blueberries and rosemary with the simple syrup, taking care not to overpress the rosemary. Add the brandy, the crème de violette, the lemon juice, and ice and shake well. Strain into a double old fashioned glass with ice. Serve garnished with skewered blueberries.

YIELD: 1 COCKTAIL

BLUEBIRD ▼

I came across this drink in my copy of Café Royal Cocktail Book *(1937), written by and for the members of the UK Bartenders Guild. I was startled to find about a dozen recipes calling for blue curaçao. Blue curaçao is a liqueur that puts me in mind of spring break in Daytona, but apparently it has a pedigree, and lucky for me, I had a bottle deep in the recesses of my liquor cabinet.*

1½ OUNCES (45 mL) VODKA

½ OUNCE (15 mL) BLUE CURAÇAO

½ OUNCE (15 mL) FRESH LEMON JUICE

¼ OUNCE (8 mL) MARASCHINO LIQUEUR

BRANDIED CHERRY FLAG (FOR GARNISH)

Combine the ingredients in a cocktail shaker filled with ice. Shake well. Strain into a chilled coupe and serve garnished with a brandied cherry flag.

YIELD: 1 COCKTAIL

BOBBY BURNS

"One of the very best Whisky cocktails," says The Savoy Cocktail Book, *"a very fast mover on St. Andrew's Day." I just love the way the smoky Scotch plays with the herbal Benedictine, and there is a welcome silky sweetness that coats the tongue. You don't need to wait till November 30 (which is St. Andrew's Day, you know) to enjoy this.*

2 OUNCES (60 mL) SCOTCH WHISKY

¾ OUNCE (23 mL) SWEET VERMOUTH

½ OUNCE (15 mL) BENEDICTINE

LEMON PEEL (FOR GARNISH)

Combine the ingredients in a cocktail shaker filled with ice. Stir well. Strain into a chilled coupe and serve garnished with a healthy slice of lemon peel.

YIELD: 1 COCKTAIL

BOMBAY COCKTAIL #3

Bombay Cocktail and Bombay Cocktail #2 both appear in The Savoy Cocktail Book. *What they have in common with my Bombay Cocktail #3 is that none of them have anything whatsoever to do with Bombay.*

1½ OUNCES (45 mL) BRANDY

¾ OUNCE (23 mL) ORANGE LIQUEUR

½ OUNCE (15 mL) SWEET VERMOUTH

¼ OUNCE (8 mL) DRY VERMOUTH

¼ OUNCE (8 mL) FRESH LEMON JUICE

⅛ OUNCE (4 mL) ABSINTHE

LEMON TWIST (FOR GARNISH)

Combine the ingredients in a cocktail shaker filled with ice. Shake well. Strain into a chilled coupe and serve garnished with a lemon twist.

YIELD: 1 COCKTAIL

BOULEVARDIER

2 OUNCES (60 ML) RYE

1 OUNCE (30 ML) CAMPARI

1 OUNCE (30 ML) SWEET VERMOUTH

LEMON TWIST (FOR GARNISH)

Combine the ingredients in a cocktail shaker filled with ice. Stir well. Strain into a chilled coupe and serve garnished with a lemon twist.

YIELD: 1 COCKTAIL

BOURBON BLUES

6–8 BLUEBERRIES (PLUS MORE FOR GARNISH)

2 FRESH BASIL LEAVES

¾ OUNCE (23 ML) TURBINADO SYRUP (SEE PAGE 27)

2 OUNCES (60 ML) BOURBON

¾ OUNCE (23 ML) FRESH LEMON JUICE

In a sturdy glass or cocktail shaker, use a muddling tool or the end of a wooden spoon to crush and mix the blueberries, basil, and turbinado syrup. Add the bourbon, the lemon juice, and ice; shake well. Strain into double old fashioned glass and top with crushed ice. Garnish with skewered blueberries.

YIELD: 1 COCKTAIL

BRANDY ALEXANDER

1 OUNCE (30 ML) BRANDY

1 OUNCE (30 ML) RUM CREAM LIQUEUR*

1 OUNCE (30 ML) CHOCOLATE LIQUEUR

1 EGG WHITE

1 WHOLE NUTMEG (FOR GARNISH)

Dry shake one egg white (see page 35). Add the remaining ingredients and ice to the cocktail shaker and shake vigorously a second time. Strain into a chilled coupe and serve garnished with ground nutmeg.

*Rum cream is more spice-and-vanilla based than Irish whiskey cream and pairs well with egg. Substitute Irish cream if you must (but omit the chocolate liqueur) for a less complex but still tasty cocktail.

YIELD: 1 COCKTAIL

BRANDY FIX

2 OUNCES (60 ML) BRANDY

1 OUNCE (30 ML) FRESH LIME JUICE

1 OUNCE (30 ML) PINEAPPLE SYRUP (SEE PAGE 148)

¼ OUNCE (8 ML) YELLOW CHARTREUSE

4 OUNCES (120 ML) CLUB SODA

ORANGE PEEL (FOR GARNISH)

Pour the brandy, lime juice, pineapple syrup, and chartreuse into a tall collins glass filled with ice. Top with the club soda and serve garnished with an orange peel twist.

YIELD: 1 COCKTAIL

BREAKFAST NEGRONI

¾ OUNCE (23 ML) GIN

¾ OUNCE (23 ML) CAMPARI

½ OUNCE (15 ML) SWEET VERMOUTH

¾ OUNCE (23 ML) BLOOD ORANGE JUICE

ORANGE PEEL (FOR GARNISH)

Combine the ingredients in a cocktail shaker filled with ice. Shake well. Strain into a double rocks glass filled with ice and serve garnished with an orange peel twist.

YIELD: 1 COCKTAIL

BROADWAY GYPSY ▾

1½ ounces (45 mL) vodka

¾ ounce (23 mL) ginger liqueur

½ ounce (15 mL) fresh lime juice

¼ ounce (8 mL) simple syrup

7–8 fresh raspberries (plus more for garnish)

3–4 ounces (90–120 mL) club soda

Pour the vodka, ginger liqueur, lime juice, simple syrup, and raspberries into an empty cocktail shaker. (This is a good opportunity to use broken and bruised berries.) Fill ¾ full with ice. Shake well, being sure to bruise the fruit. Using a Hawthorne strainer, strain into a highball glass filled with ice, top with the club soda, and serve garnished with skewered berries.

YIELD: 1 COCKTAIL

BRONX

This drink's lightly refreshing and mild taste is anything but the Bronx. I lived about four blocks from the Bronx. This is more New Rochelle.

1½ OUNCES (45 mL) GIN

¾ OUNCE (23 mL) SWEET VERMOUTH

¾ OUNCE (23 mL) DRY VERMOUTH

1 OUNCE (30 mL) ORANGE JUICE

Combine the ingredients in a cocktail shaker filled with ice. Shake well. Strain into a chilled coupe and serve ungarnished.

YIELD: 1 COCKTAIL

BROWN DERBY

Although it might appear this drink was named for the famous Hollywood restaurant, its origin lies in another 1930s hotspot, the Vendome Club. My version of this classic uses a honey-infused liqueur, which balances the cocktail with less sweetness than a honey syrup.

2 OUNCES (60 mL) RYE

1 OUNCE (30 mL) HONEY LIQUEUR

1 OUNCE (30 mL) FRESH GRAPEFRUIT JUICE

GRAPEFRUIT PEEL (FOR GARNISH)

Combine the ingredients in a cocktail shaker filled with ice. Shake well. Strain into a chilled coupe and serve garnished with a grapefruit peel twist.

YIELD: 1 COCKTAIL

BURGUNDY MULE

2 OUNCES (60 mL) GIN

½ OUNCE (15 mL) CRÈME DE CASSIS

½ OUNCE (15 mL) FRESH LEMON JUICE

3-4 OUNCES (90-120 mL) GINGER BEER

LEMON WEDGE (FOR GARNISH)

Combine the gin, crème de cassis, and lemon juice in a tall glass filled with ice. Top with the ginger beer. Stir and serve garnished with a lemon wedge.

YIELD: 1 COCKTAIL

CAIPIRINHA

2 TEASPOONS GRANULATED SUGAR

1 LIME, QUARTERED

2 OUNCES (60 mL) CACHAÇA

LIME WEDGE (FOR GARNISH)

In a sturdy glass or cocktail shaker, muddle the lime quarters with the sugar. Add the cachaça and ice and shake well. Empty the entire contents of the mixing glass into a double old fashioned glass and serve garnished with a lime wedge.

YIELD: 1 COCKTAIL

CALVADOS COCKTAIL

1½ OUNCES (45 mL) CALVADOS

¾ OUNCE (23 mL) ORANGE LIQUEUR

1½ OUNCES (45 mL) FRESH ORANGE JUICE

2 DASHES ORANGE BITTERS

ORANGE PEEL (FOR GARNISH)

Combine the ingredients in a cocktail shaker filled with ice. Shake well. Strain into a chilled coupe and serve garnished with an orange peel.

YIELD: 1 COCKTAIL

CAPE CODDER (AND PALS)

In my mind, the Cape Codder is synonymous with the 1980s. I served my share of these to big-haired Jersey girls wearing floral print dresses paired with post-work Reeboks. I was surprised to learn that Trader Vic claimed this drink as his own (in two separate books, under two separate names) and we can even find a recipe dating back to 1944. So, snob that I am, I now appreciate it more. Simple alternate versions* are also popular.

1½ OUNCES (45 mL) VODKA

CRANBERRY JUICE

3–4 OUNCES (90–120 mL) CLUB SODA (OPTIONAL)

LIME WEDGE (FOR GARNISH)

Combine the vodka and cranberry juice in a tall glass filled with ice. Top with club soda if desired. Serve garnished with a lime wedge.

*Add a splash of pineapple juice to this recipe for a Baybreeze; add a splash of grapefruit juice for a Seabreeze; add a splash of orange juice for a Madras.

YIELD: 1 COCKTAIL

CARMEN'S VERANDA

1½ ounces (45 mL) mezcal

½ ounce (15 mL) Galliano

1 ounce (30 mL) pineapple juice

½ ounce (15 mL) fresh lime juice

2 dashes orange bitters

3-4 ounces (90-120 mL) ginger beer

Grilled pineapple (for garnish)

Combine the mezcal, Galliano, pineapple juice, lime juice, and orange bitters in a cocktail shaker filled with ice. Shake well. Strain into a tall glass filled with ice. Top with the ginger beer. Serve garnished with a slice of grilled pineapple.

YIELD: 1 COCKTAIL

CELERY MARY

As a long-time resident of Manhattan, I have a soft spot in my heart for a good deli and Dr. Brown's sodas. The caraway characteristics in the aquavit add depth to this unsual and surprisingly fresh take on the Bloody Mary.

Celery salt

3 cherry tomatoes

½ tablespoon diced fresh green bell pepper

½ tablespoon diced fresh yellow bell pepper

Dash Tabasco sauce

½ ounce (15 mL) fresh lemon juice

1½ ounces (45 mL) aquavit

Dr. Brown's Cel-Ray Soda*

Celery (for garnish)

Rim a collins glass with celery salt and set aside. In a sturdy glass or cocktail shaker, muddle the cherry tomatoes, green bell pepper, yellow bell pepper, and Tabasco with the lemon juice. Add the aquavit and ice and shake well. Strain into the salt-rimmed glass. Fill glass with ice and top with the soda. Serve garnished with a thin slice of celery stalk.

*Dr. Brown's sodas are staples in NYC delis and can also be found in boutique supermarkets. Should you be unable to get your hands on them, substitute ginger ale with a pinch of crushed celery seed.

YIELD: 1 COCKTAIL

CHAMPAGNE COCKTAIL

1 SUGAR CUBE

3 DASHES ANGOSTURA AROMATIC BITTERS

1 OUNCE (30 ML) BRANDY

1 (750-ML) BOTTLE SPARKLING WINE OR PROSECCO

Soak the sugar cube in the bitters and add it to an empty champagne flute. Add the brandy, top with the sparkling wine, and serve ungarnished.

YIELD: 1 COCKTAIL

CHAMPS-ÉLYSÉES

1½ OUNCES (45 ML) VS BRANDY

½ OUNCE (15 ML) GREEN CHARTREUSE

¼ OUNCE (8 ML) FRESH LEMON JUICE

¼ TEASPOON SIMPLE SYRUP

2 DASHES ANGOSTURA AROMATIC BITTERS

Combine the ingredients in a cocktail shaker filled with ice. Shake well. Strain into a chilled coupe and serve ungarnished.

YIELD: 1 COCKTAIL

CHARTREUSE SWIZZLE

This is a great example of a "new classic cocktail" with all the elements of a vintage drink that's been around forever. Only recently created by Marco Dionysos, s the Chartreuse Swizzle is one that bartenders and bloggers suck down as the bar empties out. As Bermuda's national drink, a "swizzle" is a rum-and-citrus libation served over cracked ice and named for the special pronged stick used to stir it. You can use a shaker if you can't find yours.

1¼ OUNCES (38 ML) GREEN CHARTREUSE

½ OUNCE (15 ML) VELVET FALERNUM

1 OUNCE (30 ML) PINEAPPLE JUICE

¾ OUNCE (23 ML) FRESH LIME JUICE

FRESH NUTMEG (FOR GARNISH)

FRESH MINT (FOR GARNISH)

Combine the ingredients in a cocktail shaker filled with ice. Shake well. Strain into a collins glass filled with crushed ice. Serve with a straw, garnished with ground nutmeg and fresh mint.

YIELD: 1 COCKTAIL

CHAT NOIR

Our bartender, Carol, whipped this up one night for a Benedictine-loving client who proclaimed it "vodka and Red Bull for grownups." It's a fair description. Presented neat in a double rocks glass, the Chat Noir's deep complexion, slight foamy head, and caffeine kick are all pretty bad-ass.

¾ OUNCE (23 mL) BENEDICTINE

¾ OUNCE (23 mL) ORANGE LIQUEUR

2 OUNCES (60 mL) COLD COFFEE

ORANGE PEEL (FOR GARNISH)

Combine the ingredients in a cocktail shaker filled with ice. Shake well. Strain into a double rocks glass without ice. Rim the glass with the orange peel, express the oils over the top of the cocktail, discard the peel, and serve.

YIELD: 1 COCKTAIL

CHERRY SMASH

5-6 BRANDIED CHERRIES (PLUS MORE FOR GARNISH) (SEE PAGE 150)

1 TEASPOON BRANDIED CHERRY JUICE

¾ OUNCE (23 mL) FRESH LEMON JUICE

2 OUNCES (60 mL) BRANDY

1 OUNCE (30 mL) CHERRY KIRSCH

In a sturdy glass or cocktail shaker, use a muddling tool or the end of a wooden spoon to crush and mix the brandied cherries and lemon juices. Add the brandy, the kirsch, and ice; shake well. Strain into a double old fashioned glass with ice. Garnish with a brandied cherry.

YIELD: 1 COCKTAIL

CHILCANO DE PISCO

A classic drink from Peru, the simple and fresh tasting Chilcano de Pisco should not be confused with Chilcano de Pescado, which is fish soup.

> 2 OUNCES (60 mL) PISCO
>
> ½ OUNCE (15 mL) FRESH KEY LIME JUICE
>
> 3–4 OUNCES (90–120 mL) GINGER ALE
>
> 2 DASHES ANGOSTURA AROMATIC BITTERS
>
> KEY LIME WHEEL (FOR GARNISH)

Combine the pisco and key lime juice in a tall glass filled with ice. Top with the ginger ale. Splash the bitters over the ice. Serve unstirred and garnished with a key lime wheel.

YIELD: 1 COCKTAIL

CHOCOLATE VELVET

The Black Velvet was served to a mourning Great Britain after the death of Queen Victoria's husband, Prince Albert. It's a surprisingly tasty mix of Guinness Stout and champagne. I'm using a chocolate stout (choose your favorite; the bigger and more chocolaty, the better) and sparkling wine.

> 2 DASHES ORANGE BITTERS
>
> 4 OUNCES (120 mL) CHOCOLATE STOUT
>
> 3–4 OUNCES (90–120 mL) SPARKLING WINE OR PROSECCO
>
> ORANGE PEEL (FOR GARNISH)

Splash the orange bitters into a tall chilled collins glass; swirl the bitters to coat the glass and discard the remainder. Pour the stout into the glass. Top with the chilled sparkling wine. Serve garnished with an orange peel twist.

YIELD: 1 COCKTAIL

CLAM DIGGER

This drink freaks people out. Not Canadians, but generally everyone else. This is one of the brunch drinks I strong-arm my guests into trying, and they are inevitably delighted by its seaside freshness. In Canada they use Motts Clamato Juice specifically for this drink and call it the Bloody Caesar.

OLD BAY SEASONING

2 OUNCES (60 mL) VODKA

3 OUNCES (90 mL) TOMATO JUICE

1 OUNCE (30 mL) CLAM JUICE

FRESH PARSLEY (FOR GARNISH)

LEMON WEDGE (FOR GARNISH)

Rim a collins glass with Old Bay Seasoning and set aside. Combine the vodka, tomato juice, and clam juice in a cocktail shaker filled with ice. Pour the contents of the shaker into a second mixing glass and repeat back and forth until chilled. Empty the entire contents of the mixing glass into the spice-rimmed collins glass and top with ice if necessary. Stir and serve garnished with a lemon wedge and fresh parsley.

YIELD: 1 COCKTAIL

CLOVER CLUB

Even with its feminine appearance, this pre-Prohibition cocktail was a favorite for gentlemen's club members of the "oak-paneled lounge" set. Adding ½ ounce (15 mL) of applejack adds quite a kick and transforms the Clover Club into a much stronger, livelier, more masculine drink with a new name. What is this ballsier brother called? A Pink Lady.

1 EGG WHITE

4 OR 5 RASPBERRIES

2 OUNCES (60 mL) GIN

½ OUNCE (15 mL) SIMPLE SYRUP

½ OUNCE (15 mL) FRESH LEMON JUICE

Dry shake the egg white with the raspberries (see page 35). Add the remaining ingredients and ice to a cocktail shaker and shake vigorously a second time. Double strain into a chilled coupe and serve ungarnished.

YIELD: 1 COCKTAIL

COFFEE COCKTAIL ➤

Disclaimer: This drink's name is a lie; it contains no actual coffee. However, when done properly it looks like coffee, and the brandy and port impart a lovely warmth. I add a touch of chocolate liqueur to mine, which is more for depth of flavor than sweetness.

1 WHOLE EGG

1½ OUNCES (45 ML) BRANDY

1½ OUNCES (45 ML) RUBY PORT

½ OUNCE (15 ML) SIMPLE SYRUP

¼ OUNCE (8 ML) CHOCOLATE LIQUEUR

WHOLE NUTMEG (FOR GARNISH)

Dry shake the egg (see page 35). Add the remaining ingredients and ice to the cocktail shaker and shake vigorously a second time. Strain into a chilled coupe and serve garnished with a dusting of freshly ground nutmeg.

YIELD: 1 COCKTAIL

CORA SUE COLLINS

I thought it appropriate to name this fresh and easy Collins after a child actress who became famous at the repeal of Prohibition. Coincidentally, she appeared in the 1941 remake of Blood and Sand, *also the name of one of my favorite cocktails (page 53).*

4 OR 5 FRESH MINT LEAVES

½ OUNCE (15 ML) FRESH LEMON JUICE

1 OUNCE (30 ML) VODKA

1 OUNCE (30 ML) ELDERFLOWER LIQUEUR

4-5 OUNCES (120-150 ML) CLUB SODA

1 SPRIG FRESH MINT (FOR GARNISH)

In a sturdy glass or cocktail shaker, muddle the mint leaves with the lemon juice. Add the vodka, the elderflower liqueur, and ice and shake well. Strain into a collins glass filled with ice and top with club soda. Serve garnished with a sprig of fresh mint.

YIELD: 1 COCKTAIL

CORPSE REVIVER #2

1½ ounces (45 mL) gin

¾ ounce (23 mL) Grand Marnier

¾ ounce (23 mL) Lillet Blanc

¾ ounce (23 mL) fresh lemon juice

3 drops absinthe*

Brandied cherry (for garnish)

Combine the ingredients in a cocktail shaker filled with ice. Shake well. Strain into a chilled coupe, and serve garnished with a brandied cherry.

For better portion control, pour a few drops of absinthe onto a spoon rather than directly into the cocktail shaker; for best control, use an eyedropper.

YIELD: 1 COCKTAIL

CUBA LIBRE

Zest of ½ lime

1½ ounces (45 mL) light rum

Juice of ½ lime

3-4 ounces (90-120 mL) cola

Zest the lime half into a tall collins glass. Add the rum, the lime juice, the spent lime hull, and ice, and stir. Top with cola and serve.

YIELD: 1 COCKTAIL

DAIQUIRI

Classic. Simple. So wonderful that people couldn't help but mess with it. Mix your guests one of these and you'll understand that there's no need to improve it with bastardizations of frozen berries.

2 ounces (60 mL) light rum

1 ounce (30 mL) fresh lime juice

½ ounce (15 mL) simple syrup

Combine the ingredients in a cocktail shaker filled with ice. Shake well. Strain into a chilled coupe and serve garnished with a lime wheel.

YIELD: 1 COCKTAIL

DANISH MARY

GROUND FENNEL

KOSHER SALT

1 SPRIG FRESH DILL (PLUS MORE FOR GARNISH)

1 TEASPOON GRATED WHITE ONION

¼ OUNCE (8 mL) FRESH LEMON JUICE

1½ OUNCES (45 mL) AQUAVIT

3 OUNCES (90 mL) TOMATO JUICE

2 DASHES TABASCO SAUCE

FRESH GROUND BLACK PEPPER

Mix equal parts ground fennel and kosher salt in a shallow dish to make a rimming spice. Moisten the outer rim of a double rocks glass with lemon and coat the outside of the glass in the fennel salt. Set aside. In a sturdy glass or cocktail shaker, lightly muddle the dill and the white onion with the lemon juice. Add the aquavit, tomato juice, Tabasco, 2 grinds of black pepper, and ice, and shake well. Strain into the rimmed double rocks glass filled with ice. Serve garnished with fresh dill.

YIELD: 1 COCKTAIL

DARK AND STORMY

Perfect example of how using the perfect ingredients makes for the perfect cocktail. In my opinion, this highball, trademarked by Gosling's, is best with the original ingredients and no garnish. Don't bother making one if you don't have a spicy ginger beer. If you do, then you might as well make two, because the first always disappears quickly.

1½ OUNCES (45 mL) GOSLING'S BLACK SEAL RUM

BARRITT'S GINGER BEER

Add the rum to a tall glass filled with ice. Top with ginger beer and serve ungarnished. It doesn't need the lime that many people will add.

YIELD: 1 COCKTAIL

DARK LADY

The Savoy's White Lady (page 141) is all about light. It made me want to keep the original idea and measurements but play in the dark. Galliano adds just the right anise-accented weight to this Dark Lady.

1½ ounces (45 mL) Gosling's Black Seal Rum

1 ounce (30 mL) Galliano

1 ounce (30 mL) fresh lime juice

Lime wheel (for garnish)

Combine the ingredients in a cocktail shaker filled with ice. Shake well. Strain into a chilled coupe and serve garnished with a lime wheel.

YIELD: 1 COCKTAIL

DESERT HEALER

In my gin-induced dream, Deano, Frank, Sammy, and I enjoy these poolside at the Flamingo as the dames look on.

1½ ounces (45 mL) gin

½ ounce (15 mL) Cherry Heering

1½ ounces (45 mL) orange juice

3-4 ounces (90-120 mL) ginger beer

Combine the gin, Cherry Heering, and orange juice in a cocktail shaker filled with ice. Shake well. Strain into a tall glass filled with ice, top with ginger beer, and serve ungarnished (although I wouldn't fault you for a little paper umbrella, if you are so inclined).

YIELD: 1 COCKTAIL

DESHLER

2 ounces (60 mL) bourbon

1½ ounces (45 mL) Lillet Rouge

½ ounce (15 mL) orange liqueur

Orange slice

2 dashes Peychaud's Bitters

Orange peel (for garnish)

Combine the ingredients (including the orange slice) in a cocktail shaker. Fill with ice. Stir well, being sure to bruise the fruit. Strain into a chilled coupe and serve garnished with an orange peel.

YIELD: 1 COCKTAIL

EARL OF CHATHAM

1½ OUNCES (45 mL) LILLET BLANC

½ OUNCE (15 mL) GRAND MARNIER

½ OUNCE (15 mL) MARASCHINO LIQUEUR

¼ OUNCE (8 mL) FRESH LIME JUICE

2 DASHES ORANGE BITTERS

BRANDIED CHERRY (FOR GARNISH)

Combine the ingredients in a cocktail shaker filled with ice. Shake well. Strain into a chilled coupe and serve garnished with a brandied cherry.

YIELD: 1 COCKTAIL

EAST SIDE

I thought I developed this drink for our lakeside wedding reception. In studying recipes one day, I was surprised to see that the recipe has been around forever… with a better name.

2 THICK SLICES CUCUMBER

4 FRESH MINT LEAVES (PLUS MORE FOR GARNISH)

¾ OUNCE (23 mL) MINT SYRUP (SEE ROSEMARY SYRUP, PAGE 148)

2 OUNCES (60 mL) GIN (HENDRICK'S PREFERRED)

1 OUNCE (30 mL) FRESH LIME JUICE

In a sturdy glass or cocktail shaker, muddle the cucumber and mint leaves with the mint syrup. Add the gin, lime juice, and ice and shake well. Strain into a double old fashioned glass with ice. Serve garnished with fresh mint.

YIELD: 1 COCKTAIL

EASTERN SIN ▲

1½ ounces (45 mL) Scotch whisky

1 ounce (30 mL) Cherry Heering

½ ounce (15 mL) orange liqueur

½ ounce (15 mL) sweet vermouth

½ ounce (15 mL) fresh pineapple juice

Fresh pineapple wedge (for garnish)

Combine the ingredients in a cocktail shaker filled with ice. Shake well. Strain into a chilled coupe and serve garnished with a pineapple wedge.

YIELD: 1 COCKTAIL

EL DIABLO ▲

½ LIME

2 OUNCES (60 mL) SILVER TEQUILA

½ OUNCE (15 mL) WHITE GRAPE JUICE

½ OUNCE (15 mL) CRÈME DE CASSIS

GINGER ALE

Juice the lime half with a citrus squeezer, reserving the inverted hull. Pour the tequila, grape juice, and lime juice into a tall collins glass filled with ice. Top with ginger ale to about ½ inch (13 mm) from the top of glass. Stir gently. Place the inverted lime hull into the top of the cocktail, rind side up, and fill the "lime bowl" with crème de cassis. Serve immediately with a straw.

YIELD: 1 COCKTAIL

EL PRESIDENTE

1½ OUNCES (45 ML) LIGHT RUM

1 OUNCE (30 ML) DRY VERMOUTH

¼ OUNCE (8 ML) ORANGE LIQUEUR

½ TEASPOON GRENADINE (SEE PAGE 146)

ORANGE PEEL (FOR GARNISH)

Combine the ingredients in a cocktail shaker filled with ice. Shake well. Strain into a chilled coupe and serve garnished with a flamed orange peel.

YIELD: 1 COCKTAIL

ELDERFLOWER GIMLET

2¼ OUNCES (68 ML) GIN

1 OUNCE (30 ML) ELDERFLOWER LIQUEUR

¾ OUNCE (23 ML) FRESH LIME JUICE

LIME WHEEL, THINLY SLICED (FOR GARNISH)

Combine the ingredients in a cocktail shaker filled with ice. Shake well. Strain into a chilled coupe and serve garnished with a floating lime wheel.

YIELD: 1 COCKTAIL

ELKS OWN

At the Whistler, one of Chicago's best craft cocktail bars, I was immediately annoyed at learning of the Elks Own, a drink all the cool kids except me knew about. I could give you the recipe from 1901, but Paul McGee's update is pretty awesome.

¼ OUNCE (8 ML) WALNUT LIQUEUR (FOR RINSE)

1 EGG WHITE

1½ OUNCES (45 ML) BOURBON

½ OUNCE (15 ML) RUBY PORT

¼ OUNCE (8 ML) CYNAR

½ OUNCE (15 ML) FRESH LEMON JUICE

½ OUNCE (15 ML) SIMPLE SYRUP

Rinse a chilled coupe with the walnut liqueur and set aside. Dry shake the egg white (see page 35). Add the remaining ingredients and ice to the cocktail shaker and shake vigorously a second time. Strain into the walnut liqueur–rinsed coupe. Serve ungarnished.

YIELD: 1 COCKTAIL

EMBASSY COCKTAIL

¾ OUNCE (23 mL) BRANDY

¾ OUNCE (23 mL) DEMERARA OR DARK RUM

¾ OUNCE (23 mL) ORANGE LIQUEUR

½ OUNCE (15 mL) FRESH LIME JUICE

DASH ANGOSTURA AROMATIC BITTERS

LIME WEDGE (FOR GARNISH)

Combine the ingredients in a cocktail shaker filled with ice. Shake well. Strain into a chilled coupe and serve garnished with a lime wedge.

YIELD: 1 COCKTAIL

FENNEL RICKEY

The day Dan and I arrived to teach a class in Tuscany, we ran in different directions. He started off to the market for fresh eggs for pasta, and I started pulling fennel from the yard and stuffing it into a discarded oversized wine jug. When he got back, I had already filled my bottle with fennel fronds and gin. He could talk all he wanted about homemade gnocchi, but I had already planned an end-of-the-week cocktail…I win.

1½ OUNCES (45 mL) FENNEL-INFUSED GIN (SEE PAGE 145)

2 OUNCES (60 mL) FRESH BLOOD ORANGE JUICE

½ OUNCE (15 mL) FRESH LEMON JUICE

3-4 OUNCES (90-120 mL) CLUB SODA

FRESH FENNEL (FOR GARNISH)

Combine the gin, blood orange juice, and lemon juice in a cocktail shaker filled with ice. Shake well. Strain into a tall glass filled with ice. Top with club soda. Serve garnished with a fennel frond.

YIELD: 1 COCKTAIL

FIDDLERS THREE

1 STRAWBERRY

¼ OUNCE (8 ML) SIMPLE SYRUP

1½ OUNCES (45 ML) BOURBON

¼ OUNCE (8 ML) FERNET BRANCA

½ OUNCE (15 ML) ORANGE JUICE

½ OUNCE (15 ML) PINEAPPLE JUICE

FRESH FRUIT (FOR GARNISH)

In a sturdy glass or cocktail shaker, muddle the strawberry and simple syrup. Add the bourbon, Fernet Branca, orange and pineapple juices, and ice, and shake well. Strain into a double old fashioned glass with ice. Serve garnished with fresh fruit.

YIELD: 1 COCKTAIL

FOG CUTTER

What makes a tiki cocktail like the Fog Cutter unusual is its use of three base spirits (rum, gin, and brandy). It's another cocktail from Mai Tai creator Victor "Trader Vic" Bergeron, and the combination seems to reflect his own personality. As a pioneer in theme chain establishments, Trader Vic is a hard-shelled, hardworking guy who is equal parts innovating restaurateur, mixologist, and storyteller. And his quote on the spirits used in this tasty refresher? "Fog Cutter, hell. After two of these, you won't even see the stuff."

2 OUNCES (60 ML) LIGHT RUM

1 OUNCE (30 ML) BRANDY

½ OUNCE (15 ML) GIN

1 OUNCE (30 ML) ORGEAT SYRUP (SEE PAGE 148)

1 OUNCE (30 ML) ORANGE JUICE

2 OUNCES (60 ML) LEMON JUICE

½ OUNCE (15 ML) OLOROSO SHERRY

FRESH TROPICAL FRUIT (FOR GARNISH)

Combine all the ingredients except the sherry in a cocktail shaker filled with ice. Shake well. Strain into a tall glass filled with crushed ice. Slowly pour the sherry over the top layer of ice to create a float over the surface of the cocktail. Serve with a straw and garnished festively with your tropical fruit of choice.

YIELD: 1 COCKTAIL

GIMLET

British sailors were ordered to drink lime juice as a precaution against scurvy. It is argued that a certain General Gimlette found that adding gin would preserve the lime juice over long voyages, with the added benefit of making it more palatable to the "Limeys." Of course, wet blanket Lauchlin Rose ruined the party in the late 1800s by introducing Rose's Lime Juice as a way of preserving the juice without alcohol. A true gimlet recipe calls for Rose's Lime Juice.

> LIME WEDGE
>
> 2½ OUNCES (75 mL) GIN
>
> ½ OUNCE (15 mL) ROSE'S LIME JUICE

Rim a chilled coupe with the lime wedge. Set aside. Combine the remaining ingredients in a cocktail shaker filled with ice. Stir well. Strain into the chilled coupe, squeeze the lime into the glass, drop it in, and serve.

YIELD: 1 COCKTAIL

GINGER NEGRONI

> 2 OUNCES (60 mL) GINGER LIQUEUR
>
> ½ OUNCE (15 mL) CAMPARI
>
> ¼ OUNCE (8 mL) DRY VERMOUTH
>
> 1 OUNCE (30 mL) ORANGE JUICE
>
> ORANGE PEEL (FOR GARNISH)

Combine the ingredients in a cocktail shaker filled with ice. Shake well. Strain into a rocks glass filled with ice. Serve garnished with a flamed orange peel.

YIELD: 1 COCKTAIL

GRAPEFRUIT SMASH ⋏

¼ CUP (59 mL) RUBY RED GRAPEFRUIT, PEELED AND
    ROUGHLY CHOPPED

FRESH MINT

½ OUNCE (15 mL) SIMPLE SYRUP

2 OUNCES (60 mL) CACHAÇA

In a sturdy glass or cocktail shaker, muddle the grapefruit and 4 or 5 leaves of mint
with the simple syrup. Add the cachaça and ice; shake well. Strain into a double rocks
glass filled with ice and serve garnished with a sprig of fresh mint.

YIELD: 1 COCKTAIL

GREENPOINT

The Greenpoint became my cocktail of choice one fall, but it didn't prove to be a popular seller. I think folks are wary of chartreuse.

2 OUNCES (60 ML) RYE

½ OUNCE (15 ML) GREEN CHARTREUSE

½ OUNCE (15 ML) SWEET VERMOUTH

DASH ANGOSTURA AROMATIC BITTERS

DASH ORANGE BITTERS

LEMON TWIST (FOR GARNISH)

Combine the ingredients in a cocktail shaker filled with ice. Stir well. Strain into a chilled coupe and serve garnished with a lemon twist.

YIELD: 1 COCKTAIL

GREEN SIDE

FRESH CUCUMBER

4 FRESH MINT LEAVES

½ OUNCE (15 ML) SIMPLE SYRUP

2 OUNCES (60 ML) GIN (HENDRICK'S RECOMMENDED)

½ OUNCE (15 ML) GREEN CHARTREUSE

¾ OUNCE (23 ML) LIME JUICE

CUCUMBER WHEEL (FOR GARNISH)

In a sturdy glass or cocktail shaker, muddle the cucumber and mint with the simple syrup. Add the gin, chartreuse, lime juice, and ice, and shake well. Strain into a chilled coupe and serve garnished with a floating wheel of thinly sliced cucumber.

YIELD: 1 COCKTAIL

GRENADIER

1½ OUNCES (45 ML) BRANDY

1 OUNCE (30 ML) LILLET BLANC

½ OUNCE (15 ML) GINGER LIQUEUR

DASH GRENADINE (SEE PAGE 146)

BRANDIED CHERRY FLAG (FOR GARNISH)

Combine the ingredients in a cocktail shaker filled with ice. Shake well. Strain into a chilled coupe and serve garnished with a brandied cherry flag.

YIELD: 1 COCKTAIL

GREYHOUND

1½ ounces (45 mL) vodka

3–4 ounces (90–120 mL) grapefruit juice

Combine the ingredients in a tall glass filled with ice. Serve ungarnished.*

YIELD: 1 COCKTAIL

*To make a Salty Dog, rim the glass with kosher salt.

GRILLED PEACH FRAPPE ➤

This is a spin on a recipe included in Waring's 1947 Pick Ups and Cheer Ups *from the Waring Blendor (yes, they spelled blender with an o). Not to upset you, but in a misguided attempt to trick children into eating meat, Waring had a liquid Liver Milkshake included among his recipes.*

1 large peach

3 ounces (90 mL) Southern Comfort

½ ounce (15 mL) fresh lime juice

½ ounce (15 mL) fresh lemon juice

2 teaspoons raw sugar

¼ teaspoon pure vanilla extract

1 cup (237 mL) cracked ice

Preheat the oven to 350°F (190°C). Cut the peach in half, remove the pit, and place the peach halves ungreased on a hot grill. Grill until deep checkerboard hash marks appear for the best flavor. Remove the peach halves from the grill and place them on a baking sheet in the oven for approximately 10 minutes or until a knife easily pierces the skin. Allow to cool and remove the skin with peeler.

Combine the peach and the remaining ingredients in a blender and blend on high for approximately 10–20 seconds, or until smooth. Serve immediately in chilled glasses garnished with slices of fresh peach.

YIELD: 2 COCKTAILS

HARVEY WALLBANGER

Basically a Screwdriver with herbal Galliano. And I know you know how to make a Screwdriver, but I wanted to tell you the history. The earliest mention of the Screwdriver was in a 1949 Time *magazine article that referenced American oil rig workers in the Middle East. They added vodka to small cans of orange juice and used their screwdrivers as swizzle sticks.*

1½ OUNCES (45 ML) VODKA

3 OUNCES (90 ML) FRESH ORANGE JUICE

½ OUNCE (15 ML) GALLIANO

ORANGE SLICE (FOR GARNISH)

Combine the vodka and orange juice in a tall glass filled with ice. Float the Galliano over the top of the cocktail. Serve garnished with the orange slice.

YIELD: 1 COCKTAIL

HAWAIIAN FIZZ

1 OUNCE (30 ML) DEMERARA OR DARK RUM

½ OUNCE (15 ML) AMARETTO

½ OUNCE (15 ML) COCONUT MILK

2 DASHES ORANGE BITTERS (OPTIONAL)

3-4 OUNCES (90-120 ML) ROOT BEER

ORANGE BITTERS (OPTIONAL)

Combine the rum, amaretto, and coconut milk in a cocktail shaker filled with ice (add 2 dashes orange bitters for a deeper flavor if desired). Shake well. Strain into a tall glass filled with ice. Top with root beer. Serve with a straw and garnish festively.

YIELD: 1 COCKTAIL

HEMINGWAY DAIQUIRI

2 OUNCES (60 ML) LIGHT RUM

1 OUNCE (30 ML) FRESH LIME JUICE

1 OUNCE (30 ML) FRESH GRAPEFRUIT JUICE

¾ OUNCE (23 ML) MARASCHINO LIQUEUR

LIME WEDGE (FOR GARNISH)

Combine the ingredients in a cocktail shaker filled with ice. Shake well. Strain into a double rocks glass filled with crushed ice and serve garnished with a lime wedge.

Note: To serve the cocktail frozen, put 1 cup ice into a blender along with the other ingredients. Blend on high until smooth.

YIELD: 1 COCKTAIL

HEY BUDDY

Named for Dan's Italian grandfather, whose pride and joy was the fig tree he tended in their Long Island backyard. He'd get upset when Dan ate more than his share of Jell-O puddings and shout "Hey buuuu-ddy! 'Ow many puddin' you 'ave?!"

1 ½ TEASPOONS FIG JAM

4 FRESH SAGE LEAVES (PLUS 1 FOR GARNISH)

1 ½ OUNCES (45 ML) RYE

½ OUNCE (15 ML) FERNET BRANCA

LEMON PEEL

In a sturdy glass or cocktail shaker, muddle the fig jam and sage leaves. Add the rye, the Fernet Branca, and ice and shake very well. Double strain into a chilled coupe. Express the oils of the lemon peel over the cocktail and discard the lemon peel. Slap one leaf of fresh sage between your palms to express the oils before laying it across surface of the cocktail as garnish.

YIELD: 1 COCKTAIL

HO-HO-KUS

Assuming Jerry Thomas's wonderful hard cider Jersey Cocktail is downtown Hoboken, I'm naming my sparkling wine version for affluent uptown Ho-Ho-Kus.

1 SUGAR CUBE

2 DASHES WALNUT LIQUEUR

1 ½ OUNCES (45 ML) APPLEJACK

SPARKLING WINE OR PROSECCO

LEMON PEEL, OPTIONAL (FOR GARNISH)

Soak the sugar cube in the walnut liqueur and add it to an empty champagne flute. Add the applejack and top with sparkling wine. Serve immediately, garnished with a twist of lemon peel, if desired.

YIELD: 1 COCKTAIL

HONEYMOON

This surprisingly tasty cocktail is reason enough to stock a bottle of fragrant herbal Benedictine in your liquor cabinet.

> 2 OUNCES (60 mL) APPLEJACK
> ½ OUNCE (15 mL) BENEDICTINE
> ½ OUNCE (15 mL) ORANGE LIQUEUR
> ½ OUNCE (15 mL) FRESH LEMON JUICE

Combine the ingredients in a cocktail shaker filled with ice. Shake well. Strain into a chilled coupe and serve ungarnished.

> *YIELD: 1 COCKTAIL*

HOOTS MON

> 1½ OUNCES (45 mL) SCOTCH WHISKY
> ¾ OUNCE (23 mL) LILLET BLANC
> ¾ OUNCE (23 mL) SWEET VERMOUTH
> ORANGE PEEL (FOR GARNISH)

Combine the ingredients in a cocktail shaker filled with ice. Stir well. Strain into a chilled coupe and serve garnished with flamed orange peel.

> *YIELD: 1 COCKTAIL*

HORSERADISH GIBSON ➤

This version is all steak house and supper club, baby. Grill up a big piece of meat, get your twice-baked potato going, and set some hollandiase on the burner. A little effort must be put into infusing the vodka, but no one said this was all going to be easy. This drink would be disingenuous if it were too simple.

> 1 COCKTAIL ONION
> 1 (1 x 1½-INCH [2.5 x 3.7 CM]) STRIP RARE ROAST BEEF
> 2½ OUNCES (75 mL) HORSERADISH-INFUSED VODKA (SEE PAGE 145)
> ½ OUNCE (15 mL) DRY VERMOUTH
> DASH ANGOSTURA AROMATIC BITTERS

Wrap a cocktail onion in the strip of rare roast beef and skewer with a toothpick. Set aside. Combine the remaining ingredients in a cocktail shaker filled with ice. Shake well. Strain into a chilled coupe and serve garnished with the roast beef–wrapped cocktail onion.

YIELD: 1 COCKTAIL

HORSE'S NECK

1 LEMON

2 OUNCES (60 ML) BOURBON

5–6 OUNCES (150–180 ML) GINGER ALE

With a peeler, remove the rind from the lemon in as long a spiral as you can manage. Arrange the spiral in a highball glass with a length hanging out over the rim (the horse's neck). Fill the glass with ice. Add the bourbon. Top with ginger ale. Serve with a straw.

YIELD: 1 COCKTAIL

HOT CHERRIED RUM

1 CUP (227 G) UNSALTED BUTTER

1 CUP (225 G) BROWN SUGAR

1 CUP (200 G) SUPERFINE SUGAR

½ CUP (83 G) WHOLE DRIED CHERRIES

1 OUNCE (30 ML) CHERRY HEERING

1 TEASPOON LIME ZEST

½ TEASPOON VANILLA

PINCH SALT

1 (750-ML) BOTTLE DEMERARA OR DARK RUM

LIME WHEEL (FOR GARNISH)

Melt the butter in a large saucepan over medium heat. Add the brown sugar and superfine sugar and stir to incorporate. Remove the pan from the heat, and whisk in the dried cherries, Cherry Heering, lime zest, vanilla, and salt. Let cool and store refrigerated in an airtight container.

To serve, put 2 tablespoons of the butter mixture and 2 ounces (60 mL) of rum into a warm mug. Top with boiling water and stir. Serve garnished with a lime wheel.

YIELD: 24 SERVINGS

HOT TODDY

1½ OUNCES (45 ML) RYE

1 TEASPOON ALLSPICE DRAM

3-4 OUNCES (90-120 ML) HOT APPLE CIDER

1 CINNAMON STICK (FOR GARNISH)

Combine the rye and allspice dram in a warm mug. Top with fresh hot apple cider. Stir and serve garnished with a cinnamon stick.

YIELD: 1 COCKTAIL

INCOME TAX

Look familiar? It's basically a Bronx with bitters. But in fairness, who in the Bronx isn't a little bitter around tax time?

> 1½ ounces (45 mL) gin
> ¼ ounce (8 mL) sweet vermouth
> ¼ ounce (8 mL) dry vermouth
> 1½ ounces (45 mL) orange juice
> Dash Angostura Aromatic Bitters
> Orange peel (for garnish)

Combine the ingredients in a cocktail shaker filled with ice. Shake well. Strain into a chilled coupe and serve garnished with an orange peel twist.

YIELD: 1 COCKTAIL

IRISH BLACKTHORN

> 2½ ounces (75 mL) Irish whiskey
> ½ ounce (15 mL) dry vermouth
> 2 dashes absinthe
> 2 dashes Angostura Aromatic Bitters
> Lemon twist (for garnish)

Combine the ingredients in a cocktail shaker filled with ice. Shake well. Strain into a chilled coupe and serve garnished with a lemon twist.

YIELD: 1 COCKTAIL

JACK ROSE

> 2 ounces (60 mL) applejack
> 1 ounce (30 mL) fresh lime juice
> ¾ ounce (23 mL) grenadine (see page 146)
> Orange peel (for garnish)

Combine the ingredients in a cocktail shaker filled with ice. Shake well. Strain into a chilled coupe and serve garnished with a flamed orange peel.

YIELD: 1 COCKTAIL

JAMES JOYCE

I quite enjoyed the Oriental Cocktail from The Savoy Cocktail Book, *until I tried Gary Regan's version that subs Irish whiskey for the rye.*

1½ OUNCES (45 mL) IRISH WHISKEY

¾ OUNCE (23 mL) SWEET VERMOUTH

¾ OUNCE (23 mL) ORANGE LIQUEUR

½ OUNCE (15 mL) FRESH LIME JUICE

LIME WEDGE (FOR GARNISH)

Combine the ingredients in a cocktail shaker filled with ice. Shake well. Strain into a chilled coupe and serve garnished with a lime wedge.

YIELD: 1 COCKTAIL

JERSEY COCKTAIL

¼ OUNCE (8 mL) TURBINADO SYRUP (SEE PAGE 27)

3 DASHES ANGOSTURA AROMATIC BITTERS

HARD CIDER

LEMON TWIST (FOR GARNISH)

Fill a collins glass with crushed ice. Add the turbinado syrup and bitters, and then fill the glass with hard cider. Stir until the glass becomes very cold and condensation appears. Serve garnished with a lemon twist.

YIELD: 1 COCKTAIL

KOCHI COBBLER ➤

4 DIME-SIZED SLICES FRESH GINGER

1 CAN MANDARIN ORANGES WITH SYRUP

1½ OUNCES (45 mL) GINJO SAKE

¼ OUNCE (8 mL) GALLIANO

In a sturdy glass or cocktail shaker, muddle the ginger with ¼ ounce (8 mL) of the mandarin orange syrup. Add 6 or 7 mandarin oranges, the sake, the Galliano, and ice and shake very well, being sure to bruise the fruit. Empty the entire contents of the mixing glass into a double rocks glass and serve with a straw.

YIELD: 1 COCKTAIL

LA COPA BRASILIA

3 FRESH LIME WEDGES

2 THICK CUCUMBER SLICES

¼ OUNCE (8 mL) JALAPEÑO SYRUP (SEE PAGE 147)

2 OUNCES (60 mL) CACHAÇA

½ OUNCE (15 mL) FRESH LIME JUICE

½ OUNCE (15 mL) SIMPLE SYRUP

SMOKED SEA SALT (FOR GARNISH)

In a sturdy glass or cocktail shaker, muddle the lime wedges and cucumber slices with the jalapeño syrup. Add the cachaça, the lime juice, the simple syrup, and ice, and shake well. Empty the entire contents into a double old fashioned glass. Serve garnished with a pinch of smoked sea salt.

YIELD: 1 COCKTAIL

LAST WORD

A cocktail geek's cocktail. It includes unusual spirits, embodies the "rescued from obscurity" redemption story, and is elegant in its proportions. Four equal ingredients. Perfectly balanced. A thing of beauty.

¾ OUNCE (23 mL) GIN

¾ OUNCE (23 mL) MARASCHINO LIQUEUR

¾ OUNCE (23 mL) GREEN CHARTREUSE

¾ OUNCE (23 mL) FRESH LIME JUICE

Combine the ingredients in a cocktail shaker filled with ice. Shake well. Strain into a chilled coupe and serve ungarnished.

YIELD: 1 COCKTAIL

LAUCHLIN'S LOSS ▾

1 CUCUMBER

½ OUNCE (15 mL) MINT SYRUP (SEE ROSEMARY SYRUP, PAGE 148)

2 OUNCES (60 mL) VODKA

½ OUNCE (15 mL) FRESH LIME JUICE

2 DASHES ORANGE BITTERS

In a sturdy glass or cocktail shaker, muddle 1 thick slice of cucumber with the mint syrup. Add the vodka, lime juice, orange bitters, and ice, and shake well. Strain into a chilled coupe and serve garnished with a floating cucumber wheel.

YIELD: 1 COCKTAIL

LAVENDER LADY

1½ ounces (45 mL) vodka

½ ounce (15 mL) Calvados

½ ounce (15 mL) orange liqueur

¼ ounce (8 mL) lemon juice

¼ ounce (8 mL) Crème Yvette

Orange peel (for garnish)

Combine the ingredients in a cocktail shaker filled with ice. Shake well. Strain into a chilled coupe and serve garnished with a flamed orange peel.

YIELD: 1 COCKTAIL

LEAP YEAR ➤

Full disclosure: I like the history of this cocktail, which was created by Harry Craddock for the 1928 leap year celebration, a little more than the drink itself. I was excited to serve it for leap year 2012, and I'll toast with it again in 2016.

1 ounce (30 mL) gin

½ ounce (15 mL) Grand Marnier

½ ounce (15 mL) sweet vermouth

½ ounce (15 mL) fresh lemon juice

Lemon twist (for garnish)

Combine the ingredients in a cocktail shaker filled with ice. Shake well. Strain into a chilled coupe and serve garnished with a lemon twist.

YIELD: 1 COCKTAIL

LION'S TAIL

2 ounces (60 mL) bourbon

1 ounce (30 mL) allspice dram

1 ounce (30 mL) fresh lime juice

½ ounce (15 mL) Fernet Branca

Brandied cherry flag (for garnish)

Combine the ingredients in a cocktail shaker filled with ice. Stir well. Strain into a chilled coupe and serve garnished with a brandied cherry flag.

YIELD: 1 COCKTAIL

LOGAN SQUARE

I developed this cocktail while testing out the Boulevardier (see page 58). The maraschino adds a nutty sweetness and thickens the cocktail a bit. I named it after an area in Chicago known for its beautiful boulevards.

2 OUNCES (60 mL) RYE

½ OUNCE (15 mL) CAMPARI

½ OUNCE (15 mL) MARASCHINO LIQUEUR

DASH ORANGE BITTERS

LEMON TWIST (FOR GARNISH)

Combine the ingredients in a cocktail shaker filled with ice. Shake well. Strain into a chilled coupe and serve garnished with a lemon twist.

YIELD: 1 COCKTAIL

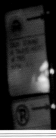

LONG IRON

We developed this tall summer drink as another way to use our delicious Green Tea-Infused Applejack and named it with a boozy nod to Arnold Palmer.

1½ OUNCES (45 ML) GREEN TEA-INFUSED APPLEJACK
(SEE PAGE 145)

LEMONADE

LEMON WHEEL (FOR GARNISH)

Add the applejack to a tall collins glass filled with ice. Top with lemonade, and serve garnished with a lemon wheel.

YIELD: 1 COCKTAIL

MAI TAI

1 OUNCE (30 ML) DEMERARA OR DARK RUM

1 OUNCE (30 ML) LIGHT RUM

½ OUNCE (15 ML) ORANGE LIQUEUR

½ OUNCE (15 ML) ORGEAT SYRUP (SEE PAGE 148)

¾ OUNCE (23 ML) FRESH LIME JUICE

¼ OUNCE (8 ML) SIMPLE SYRUP

FRESH TROPICAL FRUIT (FOR GARNISH)

Combine all the ingredients in a cocktail shaker filled with ice. Shake well. Empty the entire contents of the mixing glass into a tall glass or tiki mug and serve with a straw. Garnish festively with a tropical fruit of your choice.

YIELD: 1 COCKTAIL

MAIDEN'S BLUSH

¼ OUNCE (8 ML) ABSINTHE (FOR RINSE)

1½ OUNCES (45 ML) GIN

½ OUNCE (15 ML) LEMON JUICE

½ OUNCE (15 ML) RASPBERRY SHRUB (SEE PAGE 149)

LEMON WHEEL (FOR GARNISH)

Pour the absinthe into a chilled coupe and swirl the contents to coat the inside of the glass. Discard the excess. Combine the gin, lemon juice, and Raspberry Shrub in a cocktail shaker filled with ice. Shake well. Strain into the absinthe-rinsed coupe and serve garnished with a lemon wheel.

YIELD: 1 COCKTAIL

MAMIE TAYLOR

A deceptively delicious summer quaff. I admit to skimming past this recipe many times and kicking myself for doing so when I finally poured myself one. Be sure to use a spicy ginger beer rather than ginger ale.

2 ounces (60 mL) Scotch whisky

¼ ounce (8 mL) fresh lime juice

3-4 ounces (90-120 mL) ginger beer

Lime wedge (for garnish)

Combine the Scotch and lime juice in a tall glass filled with ice. Top with the ginger beer. Rim the glass with the lime wedge, squeeze the lime into the glass, drop it in, and serve.

YIELD: 1 COCKTAIL

MANHATTAN

2 ounces (60 mL) rye

1 ounce (30 mL) sweet vermouth

1 dash Angostura Aromatic Bitters

Brandied cherry (for garnish)

Combine the ingredients in a cocktail shaker filled with ice. Stir well. Strain into a chilled coupe and serve garnished with a brandied cherry.

YIELD: 1 COCKTAIL

MARGARITA

Kosher salt

1½ ounces (45 mL) tequila reposado

1 ounce (30 mL) orange liqueur

¾ ounce (23 mL) fresh lime juice

Lime wedge (for garnish)

Rim a chilled coupe with salt. Set aside. Combine the tequila, orange liqueur, and lime juice in a cocktail shaker filled with ice. Shake well. Strain into the chilled, salt-rimmed coupe and serve garnished with a lime wedge.

YIELD: 1 COCKTAIL

MARTINEZ

No one disagrees that this very old cocktail is the father of the Martini. Everyone disagrees, however, on the backstory. So as they argue, let's just enjoy the sweet Old Tom Gin in this wonderfully balanced winner and tune them all out.

2 OUNCES (60 mL) OLD TOM GIN

1 OUNCE (30 mL) SWEET VERMOUTH

¼ OUNCE (8 mL) MARASCHINO LIQUEUR*

2 DASHES ANGOSTURA AROMATIC BITTERS

LEMON TWIST (FOR GARNISH)

Combine the ingredients in a cocktail shaker filled with ice. Stir well. Strain into a chilled coupe and serve garnished with a lemon twist.

Some folks enjoy a straight substitution of orange liqueur for the maraschino. If you're in the mood, knock yourself out.

YIELD: 1 COCKTAIL

MARTINI (CLASSIC)

I am not even going to try to tell you the best way to make a martini, because every boozehound and their brother makes "the best martini ever." Martini ratios and methods are a matter of personal taste. However, for your edification, I am including what would be regarded as the classic recipe.

2 OUNCES (60 mL) GIN

½ OUNCE (15 mL) DRY VERMOUTH

LEMON TWIST OR OLIVE (FOR GARNISH)

Combine the ingredients in a cocktail shaker filled with ice. Stir well. Strain into a chilled coupe and serve garnished with your preference of either a lemon twist run along the rim of the glass or an olive.

YIELD: 1 COCKTAIL

MASALA RUM AND COKE ▾

"When the Coke is poured into the glass, which has a couple of teaspoons of the masala waiting to attack the liquid from the bottom up, the American drink froths up in astonished anger. The waiter stands at your booth, waiting until the froth dies down, then puts in a little more of the Coke, then waits a moment more, then pours in the rest."

Thus Suketu Mehta describes Masala Coke in Maximum City: Bombay Lost and Found. *I solved the frothing problem by adding the masala to the rum first. I solved the anger problem in the same way—I added rum.*

>   2 OUNCES (60 ML) LIGHT RUM
>   1 TEASPOON GARAM MASALA*
>   5-6 OUNCES (150-180 ML) COCA-COLA
>   LEMON WEDGE
>   FRESH MINT (FOR GARNISH)

Combine the rum and garam masala in a double old fashioned glass and stir to incorporate. Fill the glass with ice, and slowly top with the Coke. Rim the glass with the lemon wedge, squeeze the lemon into the glass, and drop it in. Serve garnished with fresh mint.

*Garam masala is a warm and earthy Indian spice blend available in Indian markets and in larger supermarkets. (You can also make your own.)

YIELD: 1 COCKTAIL

MAYFAIR

> 1 OUNCE (30 mL) GIN
>
> 1 OUNCE (30 mL) APRICOT BRANDY
>
> ¾ OUNCE (23 mL) FRESH ORANGE JUICE
>
> ¼ OUNCE (8 mL) ALLSPICE DRAM
>
> DRIED APRICOT (FOR GARNISH)

Combine the ingredients in a cocktail shaker filled with ice. Shake well. Strain into a chilled coupe and serve garnished with a dried apricot.

YIELD: 1 COCKTAIL

MICHELADA CUBANA

> TAJÍN MEXICAN SEASONING
>
> 1 TEASPOON FINELY CHOPPED JALAPEÑO
>
> 1 TEASPOON FRESH LIME JUICE
>
> 1 TEASPOON FRESH LEMON JUICE
>
> 1 TEASPOON FRESH ORANGE JUICE
>
> COLD CERVEZA (BOHEMIA OR OTHER LARGER-FLAVORED BEERS RECOMMENDED)
>
> LEMON WEDGE (FOR GARNISH)

Rim a pilsner glass with Tajín Mexican Seasoning (or salt, if you prefer) and set aside. In a sturdy glass or cocktail shaker, muddle the jalapeño with the citrus juices. Strain into the spice-rimmed pilsner. Add three or four ice cubes and top with the beer. Serve garnished with a lemon wedge.

YIELD: 1 COCKTAIL

MISTAKEN NEGRONI ▾

Milan's famed Bar Basso is responsible for this mid-century cocktail, where sparkling wine takes the place of gin. We serve it mimosa style in a champagne flute, but feel free to go the more traditional route and pour it over ice.

1 OUNCE (30 mL) CAMPARI
1 OUNCE (30 mL) SWEET VERMOUTH
1 OUNCE (30 mL) FRESH ORANGE JUICE
SPARKLING WINE OR PROSECCO
ORANGE PEEL (FOR GARNISH)

Combine the ingredients in a cocktail shaker filled with ice. Shake well. Strain into a champagne flute and top with sparkling wine. Serve garnished with a flamed orange peel.

YIELD: 1 COCKTAIL

MOJITO

FRESH MINT

¾ OUNCE (23 mL) SIMPLE SYRUP

1½ OUNCES (45 mL) LIGHT RUM

¾ OUNCE (23 mL) FRESH LIME JUICE

3-4 OUNCES (90-120 mL) CLUB SODA

In a sturdy double rocks glass, muddle 8 to 12 mint leaves with the simple syrup. Add the rum and lime juice and top with crushed ice. Stir well. Top with the club soda and serve garnished with a sprig of mint.

YIELD: 1 COCKTAIL

MONKEY GLAND

How could I not be intrigued by a drink with a name like this? After numerous failed attempts, I mixed one up using homemade grenadine. Voilà. I'll never buy a bottle again.

1½ OUNCES (45 mL) GIN

1 OUNCE (30 mL) FRESH ORANGE JUICE

1 TEASPOON GRENADINE (SEE PAGE 146)

¼ TEASPOON ABSINTHE

Combine the ingredients in a cocktail shaker filled with ice. Shake well. Strain into a chilled coupe and serve ungarnished.

YIELD: 1 COCKTAIL

MONTAUK

1½ OUNCES (45 mL) GIN

1 OUNCE (30 mL) SWEET VERMOUTH

¼ OUNCE (8 mL) YELLOW CHARTREUSE

¼ OUNCE (8 mL) SIMPLE SYRUP

DASH ORANGE BITTERS

ORANGE PEEL (FOR GARNISH)

Combine the ingredients in a cocktail shaker filled with ice. Shake well. Strain into a chilled coupe and serve garnished with a flamed orange peel.

YIELD: 1 COCKTAIL

MOSCOW MULE

Originally a marketing ploy used to help sell both ginger beer and vodka, the Moscow Mule really helped boost vodka's popularity in the United States. Part of the advertising plan was the manufacture of branded copper mugs in which to serve the drink. They're totally cool. I got my set on eBay and our son drinks his milk out of one every morning.

1¾ OUNCES (53 ML) VODKA

½ OUNCE (15 ML) FRESH LIME JUICE

3–4 OUNCES (90–120 ML) GINGER BEER

LIME WEDGE (FOR GARNISH)

Combine the vodka and lime juice in a tall glass filled with ice. Top with the ginger beer. Serve garnished with a lime wedge.

YIELD: 1 COCKTAIL

◄ MR. EDDIE'S FATHER

1 EGG WHITE

1½ OUNCES (45 ML) GIN

¾ OUNCE (23 ML) YELLOW CHARTREUSE

1 OUNCE (30 ML) FRESH GRAPEFRUIT JUICE

¼ OUNCE (8 ML) FRESH LEMON JUICE

GRAPEFRUIT TWIST (FOR GARNISH)

Dry shake the egg white (see page 35). Add the remaining ingredients and ice to the cocktail shaker and shake vigorously a second time. Strain into a chilled coupe. Serve garnished with a long, curly grapefruit twist.

YIELD: 1 COCKTAIL

NAUGHTY MISSIONARY

FRESH MINT

1½ OUNCES (45 ML) GIN

1½ OUNCES (45 ML) APRICOT BRANDY

¼ OUNCE (8 ML) FRESH LEMON JUICE

¼ OUNCE (8 ML) SIMPLE SYRUP (OPTIONAL)

In a sturdy glass or cocktail shaker, lightly muddle 3 to 4 mint leaves. Add the remaining ingredients and ice and shake well. Strain into a tiki mug filled with crushed ice. Serve garnished with a sprig of mint.

YIELD: 1 COCKTAIL

NAVY GROG

Tiki! Even the category sounds like a party. This one is adapted from Don the Beachcomber, the guy who invented not just Navy Grog but the whole idea of tiki bars.

1 OUNCE (30 mL) LIGHT RUM

1 OUNCE (30 mL) DEMERARA OR DARK RUM

1 OUNCE (30 mL) GOSLING'S BLACK SEAL RUM

1 OUNCE (30 mL) FRESH GRAPEFRUIT JUICE

1 OUNCE (30 mL) PINEAPPLE SYRUP (SEE PAGE 148)

¾ OUNCE (23 mL) FRESH LIME JUICE

¼ OUNCE (8 mL) FRESH LEMON JUICE

2 DROPS ALLSPICE DRAM

2-3 OUNCES (60-90 mL) CLUB SODA

FRESH TROPICAL FRUIT (FOR GARNISH)

Combine all the ingredients except the club soda in a cocktail shaker filled with ice. Shake well. Strain into a pilsner glass filled with crushed ice. Top with the club soda. Serve with a drinking straw and garnish festively with your tropical fruit of choice.

YIELD: 1 COCKTAIL

NORA BATTY

2 OUNCES (60 mL) BRANDY

½ OUNCE (15 mL) FRESH LIME JUICE

¼ OUNCE (8 mL) RASPBERRY SHRUB (SEE PAGE 149)

FRESH RASPBERRIES (FOR GARNISH)

Combine the ingredients in a cocktail shaker filled with ice. Shake well. Strain into a chilled coupe and serve garnished with fresh raspberries.

YIELD: 1 COCKTAIL

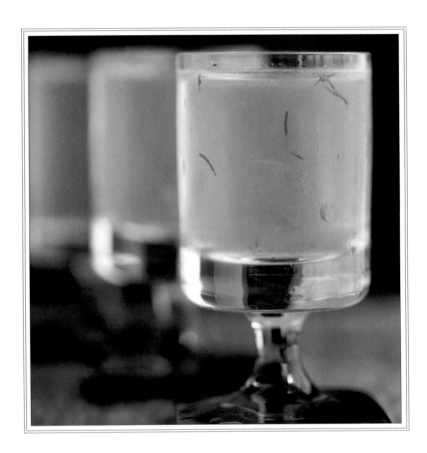

NORSE COURAGE ▲

A shot: the ultimate old-school tipple. The Swedes traditionally shoot ice-cold aquavit, the spice-laden, herbaceous Scandinavian spirit. Aquavit has a savory flavor profile of caraway, cardamom, fennel, and dill so this preparation will work great at brunch. Pour it with gravlax.

1 DILL FROND

½ OUNCE (15 mL) PICKLE BRINE

1½ OUNCES (45 mL) AQUAVIT

Muddle the dill and the pickle brine in the bottom of an empty cocktail shaker. Add the aquavit and shake well with ice. Strain into an ice-cold shot glass and serve.

YIELD: 1 SHOT

OBITUARY

    2 OUNCES (60 ML) GIN
    ¼ OUNCE (8 ML) DRY VERMOUTH
    ¼ OUNCE (8 ML) ABSINTHE

Combine the ingredients in a cocktail shaker filled with ice. Shake well. Strain into a chilled coupe and serve ungarnished.

    YIELD: 1 COCKTAIL

OH HENRY!

This drink is one of the sweeter ones I've included. I don't seek out sweet drinks, but every now and then there is definitely a place for one. I also like that the Oh Henry! comes with its own urgent punctuation that seems to suggest shouting it as you serve.

    2 OUNCES (60 ML) SCOTCH WHISKY
    ¾ OUNCE (23 ML) BENEDICTINE
    GINGER ALE
    ORANGE SLICE (FOR GARNISH)

Combine the Scotch and Benedictine in a collins glass filled with ice. Stir well. Top with ginger ale and serve garnished with an orange slice.

    YIELD: 1 COCKTAIL

OLD FASHIONED

There are many ways to make an Old Fashioned. The original method includes a bitters-soaked sugar cube and no more fruit than a lemon twist. But as far as I'm concerned, Mad Men *purchased the Old Fashioned franchise, and I'm going no more old-school than what Don Draper demands.*

    1 SUGAR CUBE (OR ½ TEASPOON GRANULATED SUGAR)
    2 DASHES ANGOSTURA AROMATIC BITTERS
    1 TEASPOON CLUB SODA
    2 OUNCES (60 ML) BOURBON OR RYE
    1 LEMON TWIST
    1 MARASCHINO CHERRY
    1 ORANGE SLICE

Muddle the sugar and bitters in the bottom of an old fashioned glass with a teaspoon of club soda. Swirl the contents to coat the inside of the glass before adding the bourbon and one large ice chunk. Squeeze in the lemon twist before adding the cherry and orange slice. Stir and serve.

YIELD: 1 COCKTAIL

OLD PAL

> 1½ ounces (45 mL) rye
>
> 1 ounce (30 mL) Campari
>
> 1 ounce (30 mL) dry vermouth

Combine the ingredients in a cocktail shaker filled with ice. Stir well. Strain into a chilled coupe and serve ungarnished.

YIELD: 1 COCKTAIL

OLD TOM PINEAPPLE COLLINS

This summery twist on the Tom Collins is pretty hard to pass up. Simply replace the pineapple syrup with simple syrup for the traditional Tom Collins.

> 1½ ounces (45 mL) Old Tom Gin
>
> 1 ounce (30 mL) pineapple syrup (see page 148)
>
> ¾ ounce (23 mL) fresh lemon juice
>
> 3-4 ounces (90-120 mL) club soda
>
> Lemon wheel and brandied cherry flag (for garnish)

Combine the gin, pineapple syrup, and lemon juice in a cocktail shaker filled with ice. Shake well. Strain into a tall glass filled with ice. Top with the club soda. Serve garnished with the lemon wheel and brandied cherry flag.

YIELD: 1 COCKTAIL

ORANGE BLOSSOM

The Orange Blossom is refreshing and just sweet enough to make you want to throw a garden party. And while you're in that garden, you might get crazy garnishing with some rosemary or lemon verbena or even thyme blossoms.

1½ OUNCES (45 ML) GIN

1½ OUNCES (45 ML) FRESH ORANGE JUICE

¼ OUNCE (8 ML) SIMPLE SYRUP

FRESH HERBS (FOR GARNISH)

Combine the ingredients in a cocktail shaker filled with ice. Shake well. Strain into a chilled coupe and serve garnished with the best available fresh herbs.

YIELD: 1 COCKTAIL

THE OTHER BROTHER

Two of my favorite liqueur brands are St. Germain Elderflower and Canton Ginger. Oddly enough, the companies are separately owned by feuding brothers. Further, their father made his fortune by introducing the raspberry liqueur Chambord to the United States. It's a shame they don't get along; I bet the drinks at their Super Bowl parties would be awesome.

1½ OUNCES (45 ML) VODKA

½ OUNCE (15 ML) ELDERFLOWER LIQUEUR

¼ OUNCE (8 ML) FRESH LEMON JUICE

¼ TEASPOON ORANGE BLOSSOM WATER

3 DASHES ORANGE BITTERS

Combine the ingredients in a cocktail shaker filled with ice. Shake well. Strain into a chilled coupe and serve ungarnished.

YIELD: 1 COCKTAIL

PEGGY'S EMERGENCY ➤

From the "because I can" category comes this drink based on a quote from Mad Men's *Peggy Olson: "You need three ingredients for a cocktail. Vodka and Mountain Dew is an emergency." I considered the gauntlet thrown.*

FRESH MINT

¼ OUNCE (8 ML) FRESH LEMON JUICE

1½ OUNCES (45 ML) PIMMS NO. 1

½ OUNCE (15 mL) VODKA

DASH ANGOSTURA AROMATIC BITTERS

3–4 OUNCES (90–120 mL) MOUNTAIN DEW

In a sturdy glass or cocktail shaker, muddle 4 mint leaves with the lemon juice. Add the Pimms, vodka, bitters, and ice and shake well. Strain into a tall glass filled with ice. Top with the Mountain Dew. Serve with a straw and garnished with fresh mint.

YIELD: 1 COCKTAIL

PEGU CLUB

My house drink, meaning if you come to my house (and you're certainly all invited) this will very likely be my standby cocktail.

> 2¼ OUNCES (68 mL) GIN
>
> 1 OUNCE (30 mL) ORANGE LIQUEUR
>
> ¾ OUNCE (23 mL) FRESH LIME JUICE
>
> 3 HEALTHY DASHES ANGOSTURA AROMATIC BITTERS
>
> LIME WEDGE (FOR GARNISH)

Rim a chilled coupe with the lime wedge. Set aside. Combine the other ingredients in a cocktail shaker filled with ice. Shake well. Strain into the chilled coupe and serve garnished with the lime wedge.

> *YIELD: 1 COCKTAIL*

PERFECT ROB ROY

The term "perfect" in mixology refers to equal parts sweet and dry vermouth. In this case, the addition of the brandied cherry juice pushes us just a bit past perfection, toward nirvana.

> 2 OUNCES (60 mL) SCOTCH WHISKY
>
> ¾ OUNCE (23 mL) SWEET VERMOUTH
>
> ¾ OUNCE (23 mL) DRY VERMOUTH
>
> ¼ TEASPOON SIMPLE SYRUP
>
> 1 TEASPOON BRANDIED CHERRY JUICE
>
> 1 TEASPOON FRESH ORANGE JUICE
>
> 10 DROPS MAPLE BITTERS*
>
> BRANDIED CHERRY FLAG (FOR GARNISH)

Combine the ingredients except the maple bitters in a cocktail shaker filled with ice. Stir well. Strain into a double rocks glass with one large ice chunk. Drip the maple bitters over the ice and serve garnished with a brandied cherry flag.

Maple bitters are available online and really bring this cocktail to a new level.

> *YIELD: 1 COCKTAIL*

PERSIMMON COBBLER

½ FRESH FUYU PERSIMMON, CHOPPED AND QUARTERED

½ OUNCE (15 ML) TURBINADO SYRUP (SEE PAGE 27)

2 OUNCES (60 ML) GOSLING'S BLACK SEAL RUM

¼ OUNCE (8 ML) ALLSPICE DRAM

ORANGE SLICE (FOR GARNISH)

In a sturdy glass or cocktail shaker, use a muddling tool to crush the persimmon with the turbinado syrup. Add the rum, the allspice dram, and ice and shake well. Empty the entire contents of the mixing glass into a double old fashioned glass. Serve garnished with an orange slice.

YIELD: 1 COCKTAIL

PHILLIPS HEAD SCREWDRIVER

This modern take on an American staple is one of my most popular drinks at Hearty, proving once again that people gravitate toward the familiar flavors of childhood. The bitter Campari and fresh lime juice will take the sugary edge off the orange soda.

2 OUNCES (60 ML) VODKA

½ OUNCE (15 ML) CAMPARI

½ OUNCE (15 ML) ORANGE LIQUEUR

½ OUNCE (15 ML) FRESH LIME JUICE

½ OUNCE (15 ML) ORANGE SODA

LIME WHEEL, THINLY SLICED

Combine the vodka, Campari, orange liqueur, and lime juice in cocktail shaker filled with ice. Shake well. Add the orange soda to the shaker and stir gently to remove some effervescence. Strain into a chilled coupe and serve garnished with a floating lime wheel.

YIELD: 1 COCKTAIL

PIMM'S CUP

Pimm's No. 1 is a gin-based liquor flavored with herbs and quinine. This recipe is for the most basic use of Pimm's No. 1; possibly England's favorite drink, if you don't count tea. On a warm summer afternoon, you'll reap massive rewards with this quintessential British cooler.

1 English cucumber

1 lemon slice

2 ounces (60 mL) Pimm's No. 1

6 ounces (180 mL) good-quality lemon soda, such as San Pellegrino Limonata

Halve an English cucumber lengthwise. Run a vegetable peeler along the length of the exposed side to create a long thin strip. Spiral the cucumber strip around the inside of a tall glass. Add the lemon slice and fill the glass with ice. Add the Pimm's and top with the lemon soda. Stir and serve.

YIELD: 1 COCKTAIL

PINK GIN

This velvet boxing glove of a drink sounds awful to Americans, just gin and bitters. Yet, it was a staple among British sailors, who drank it warm. It owes its longstanding history to Plymouth Gin, which is a must for the recipe. But do not forget to chill it… we're not actually British sailors, for God's sake.

3 ounces (90 mL) Plymouth Gin

4–6 drops Angostura Aromatic Bitters

Lemon twist (for garnish)

Combine the ingredients in a cocktail shaker filled with ice. Stir well. Strain into a chilled coupe and serve garnished with a lemon twist.

YIELD: 1 COCKTAIL

PINK SQUIRREL

I was boasting to a friend that this book contained 200 recipes and he'd be hard-pressed to name a classic cocktail that I didn't include. "Go ahead," I said, "throw out a name."

"Umm, Pink Squirrel?"

Thankfully, we hadn't gone to print yet and I was able to add this to prove him wrong.

¾ OUNCE (23 mL) CRÈME DE NOYAUX

¾ OUNCE (23 mL) WHITE CRÈME DE CACAO

½ OUNCE (15 mL) VODKA

1 OUNCE (30 mL) CREAM

½ CUP ICE

TOASTED HAZELNUTS (FOR GARNISH)

Combine the ingredients in a blender with the ice and blend on high until smooth. Pour into a chilled glass. Using a microplane, grate a toasted hazelnut directly over the cocktail as garnish. Serve immediately.

YIELD: 1 COCKTAIL

PLANTERS PUNCH

In 1848 the London magazine FUN *published a Planter's Punch recipe in verse. It starts off well enough but goes south when it rhymes "please take a" with "Jamaica." Maybe it sounds more plausible after having one.*

2 OUNCES (60 mL) DEMERARA OR DARK RUM

2 OUNCES (60 mL) PINEAPPLE JUICE

2 OUNCES (60 mL) ORANGE JUICE

½ OUNCE (15 mL) FRESH LIME JUICE

DASH GRENADINE (SEE PAGE 146)

PINEAPPLE FLAG (FOR GARNISH)

Combine all the ingredients in a cocktail shaker filled with ice. Shake well. Strain into a tall glass filled with crushed ice. Serve with a drinking straw and garnished with a pineapple flag.

YIELD: 1 COCKTAIL

POLLINATOR

If it seems like I'm including a few Crème Yvette drinks, it's because I just love its floral sweetness and I want to give you an excuse to buy a bottle. And this, my dear friends, is just a lovely excuse.

1½ OUNCES (45 ML) OLD TOM GIN

¾ OUNCE (23 ML) CRÈME YVETTE

¼ OUNCE (8 ML) ELDERFLOWER LIQUEUR

2 DASHES ORANGE BITTERS

3–4 OUNCES (90–120 ML) CLUB SODA

LEMON TWIST (FOR GARNISH)

Combine the gin, Crème Yvette, elderflower liqueur, and bitters in a collins glass filled with ice. Stir well and top with the club soda. Serve garnished with a lemon twist.

YIELD: 1 COCKTAIL

PORT WINE FLIP

Flips are a category of drinks that once contained ale, eggs, brandy, and cream and were heated with a poker hot from the fire. Although it's no longer heated, you'll find that this drink will still warm you and that it is an excellent alternative to heavy eggnog.

1 WHOLE EGG

1 OUNCE (30 ML) RUBY PORT

¾ OUNCE (23 ML) RUM CREAM LIQUEUR

¾ OUNCE (23 ML) LICOR 43*

WHOLE NUTMEG (FOR GARNISH)

Dry shake the egg (see page 35). Add the wine, the rum cream, the Licor 43, and ice to the cocktail shaker and shake vigorously a second time. Strain into a chilled coupe. Serve garnished with freshly ground nutmeg.

YIELD: 1 COCKTAIL

*Licor 43 is a rum-like Spanish liqueur with flavors of vanilla and fruit. You can substitute a fruit brandy in its place, but obtaining a bottle for your stock will not be a wasted purchase. It's a fun addition to margaritas and after-dinner drinks.

POUSSE CAFÉ ▾

Feeling fancy? A Pousse Café is an after-dinner cordial poured into three to seven distinct layers. The trick is to layer the liquids according to their density (heaviest at the bottom) without disturbing the strata or splashing on the sides of the glass. Search online for "liqueur gravity and density" to find weight charts for creating your own.

½ OUNCE (15 mL) GRENADINE (SEE PAGE 146)

½ OUNCE (15 mL) MARASCHINO LIQUEUR

½ OUNCE (15 mL) CRÈME YVETTE

Place a bar spoon into the base of a pony glass while keeping the round back side facing up. Slowly pour the grenadine over the convex back side (not down the handle) while keeping the spoon tip against or very near the inner wall of the glass. When complete, raise the spoon to just above the finished layer and repeat the process with the maraschino and finally with the Crème Yvette, slowly allowing each layer to float atop the previous layer. This takes practice so pour carefully and don't jostle the glass. Allow the layers to stabilize, and serve.

YIELD: 1 COCKTAIL

PROHIBITION

1½ ounces (45 mL) gin

1½ ounces (45 mL) Lillet Blanc

½ ounce (15 mL) apricot brandy

½ ounce (15 mL) fresh orange juice

Orange peel (for garnish)

Combine the ingredients in a cocktail shaker filled with ice. Shake well. Strain into a chilled coupe and serve garnished with an orange peel twist.

YIELD: 1 COCKTAIL

RAMOS GIN FIZZ

Some label the Ramos Gin Fizz a "difficult drink," and they're correct. Stories abound of how it must be shaken for up to twelve minutes and of New Orleans bars that had teams of "busy shaker boys" shaking to exhaustion, each handing the drink down a line until the fizz was perfect. Still, the effort is worth it for this historic beverage. And, by way of full disclosure, I use a stick blender when my team of "busy shaker boys" is off the clock.

1 egg white

2 ounces (60 mL) gin

1 ounce (30 mL) half-and-half

¼ ounce (8 mL) fresh lemon juice

¼ ounce (8 mL) fresh lime juice

1 tablespoon simple syrup

3 drops orange blossom water

3–4 ounces (90–120 mL) club soda

Orange slice (for garnish)

4 drops pure vanilla extract (for garnish)

Dry shake the egg white (see page 35). Add the gin, the half-and-half, the lemon and lime juices, the simple syrup, the orange blossom water, and ice to the cocktail shaker and shake vigorously a second time for a minimum of one minute. Alternately, blend without ice for 30 seconds using a stick blender or immersion blender. Strain into a tall glass filled with ice. Top with the club soda. Serve garnished with an orange slice and the drops of vanilla extract over the foam.

YIELD: 1 COCKTAIL

RASPBERRY BRAMBLE

2 ounces (60 mL) gin

½ ounce (15 mL) fresh lemon juice

½ ounce (15 mL) simple syrup

½ ounce (15 mL) Raspberry Shrub (see p 149)

Fresh berries (for garnish)

Combine the gin, lemon juice, and simple syrup in a cocktail shaker filled with ice. Shake well. Strain into a collins glass and top with crushed ice. Pour the Raspberry Shrub over top of the ice and let it sink slowly to the bottom. Serve with a straw, unstirred and garnished with fresh berries.

YIELD: 1 COCKTAIL

ROASTED PEAR BELLINI

1 tablespoon Roasted Pear Puree (see page 151)

1 ounce (30 mL) pear nectar

1 (750-mL) bottle sparkling wine or prosecco

Combine the pear puree and pear nectar in a chilled champagne flute. Top very slowly with sparkling wine, as you may experience fizzing. Stir gently and serve ungarnished.

YIELD: 1 COCKTAIL

ROCK AND RYE ➤

This isn't booze; it's medicine! Once used as a cure for the common cold, this distinctly American tipple can be enjoyed on the rocks, as part of a flavorful Manhattan, or added to hot water for a Toddy that will be good for what ails you. Horehound is a bitter herb known for its cough suppressant qualities, figs are loaded with B vitamins, and cloves are said to be an aphrodisiac. Don't you feel better already?

1 (750-ML) BOTTLE RYE

6 HOREHOUND CANDY DROPS

PEEL OF 1 LEMON

PEEL OF 1 ORANGE

2 DRIED FIGS

6 WHOLE CLOVES

4-INCH (10 CM) PIECE ROCK CANDY

1 OUNCE (30 ML) CHERRY SYRUP

Pour the rye into a large, wide-mouthed jar. Add the rest of the ingredients and cover. Steep for at least three days, gently shaking the contents daily. The flavor will change over time as the ingredients steep, so taste periodically, and strain and re-bottle when the flavor is to your liking. Alternately, you can keep the fruits and candy in the jar and top off with additional rye as your mixture is depleted.

YIELD: 1 (750-ML) BOTTLE

ROSABELLA'S FLING

This is a delicate drink. It needs the 6 drops of orange blossom water; it needs the caramelized oils of the orange zest. It is beautiful and earthy and demands to be served with stinky cheeses and fried olives (see page 156).

1¼ OUNCES (38 ML) GIN

1 OUNCE (30 ML) BEET JUICE*

½ OUNCE (15 ML) OLOROSO SHERRY

¼ OUNCE (8 ML) GINGER LIQUEUR

⅛ OUNCE (4 ML) ORANGE BLOSSOM WATER

ORANGE PEEL (FOR GARNISH)

Combine the ingredients in a cocktail shaker filled with ice. Shake well. Strain into a chilled coupe and serve garnished with a flamed orange peel.

*Beet juice can easily be made at home with a juicer or purchased at larger markets and health food stores for about $7.

YIELD: 1 COCKTAIL

ROSEMARY PEACH BLOW FIZZ

I know…the name, right? And the strangest thing about a Peach Blow Fizz is that the original recipe didn't even contain any peach! But mine does, and it is lightly sweet, creamy, slightly fizzy, and a terrific brunch alternative to the Mimosa.

1½ OUNCES (45 ML) OLD TOM GIN

1 OUNCE (30 ML) ROSEMARY SYRUP (SEE P 148)

1 OUNCE (30 ML) PEACH NECTAR

½ OUNCE (15 ML) HALF-AND-HALF

¼ OUNCE (8 ML) FRESH LIME JUICE

2–3 OUNCES (60–90 ML) CLUB SODA

FRESH ROSEMARY (FOR GARNISH)

Combine the gin, rosemary syrup, peach nectar, half-and-half, and lime juice in a cocktail shaker filled with ice. Shake very well. Strain into a short glass filled halfway with crushed ice and top sparingly with the club soda. Serve with a drinking straw and garnished with a sprig of fresh rosemary.

YIELD: 1 COCKTAIL

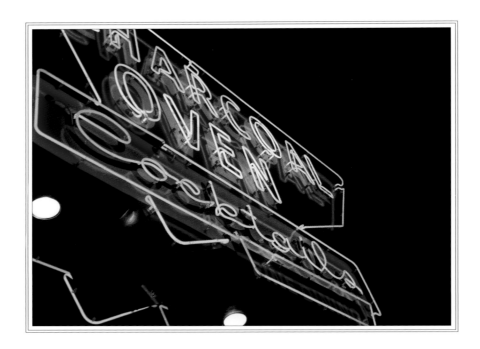

ROSEMARY RHUBARB FLIP

Fresh rhubarb

½ ounce (15 mL) fresh lime juice

1 egg white

1½ ounces (45 mL) gin

¾ ounce (23 mL) rosemary syrup (see page 148)

In a sturdy glass or cocktail shaker, muddle a 1½- to 2-inch piece of rhubarb with
the lime juice. Set aside. Dry shake the egg white (see page 35). Add the muddled
rhubarb, the gin, the rosemary syrup, and ice and shake vigorously a second time.
Strain into a collins glass with ice. Serve garnished with a thinly sliced twist of
rhubarb stalk.

YIELD: 1 COCKTAIL

RUBY KEELER

This is my recipe for what seems like a "good old-fashioned cocktail," which, coincidentally, was a hit song from the 1934 movie Wonder Bar. *Have one of these as you listen to Ruby Keeler urge you to "have a good old-fashioned cocktail with a good old-fashioned gal!" and then mix another during her big tap break.*

GRANULATED SUGAR (FOR GARNISH)

1½ OUNCES (45 ML) BRANDY

¾ OUNCE (23 ML) AQUAVIT

½ OUNCE (15 ML) FRESH LEMON JUICE

¼ OUNCE (8 ML) SIMPLE SYRUP

2 DASHES ORANGE BITTERS

Rim a chilled coupe with sugar and set aside. Combine the other ingredients in a cocktail shaker filled with ice. Shake well. Strain into the sugar-rimmed coupe and serve ungarnished.

YIELD: 1 COCKTAIL

RUSTICA

1 CANNED, PACKED-IN-SYRUP PEAR HALF

½ OUNCE (15 ML) ROSEMARY SYRUP (SEE PAGE 148)

2 OUNCES (60 ML) BOURBON

¾ OUNCE (23 ML) AMARO AVERNA

FRESH ROSEMARY (FOR GARNISH)

In a sturdy glass or cocktail shaker, muddle the pear with the rosemary syrup. Add the bourbon, the Averna, and ice and shake well. Double strain into a chilled coupe and serve garnished with fresh rosemary.

YIELD: 1 COCKTAIL

RUSTY NAIL

  2 ounces (60 mL) blended Scotch whisky

  ¾ ounce (23 mL) Drambuie

Combine the ingredients in a cocktail shaker filled with ice. Stir well.
Serve ungarnished.

  YIELD: 1 COCKTAIL

SALTY CHIHUAHUA

*Certainly the Salty Dog (a version of the Greyhound, page 82) is better known than its
Mexican cousin. But I prefer this version because tequila pairs so well with grapefruit.*

  Kosher salt (for garnish)

  1 ounce (30 mL) tequila reposado

  ½ ounce (15 mL) orange liqueur

  3–4 ounces (90–120 mL) grapefruit juice

  Grapefruit slice (for garnish)

Rim a double rocks glass with salt and fill it with ice. Combine the tequila and orange
liqueur in the salt-rimmed glass. Top with the grapefruit juice. Stir and serve garnished
with a slice of grapefruit.

  YIELD: 1 COCKTAIL

SATAN'S SISTER

  3 (1-inch [2.5-cm]) slices fresh ginger

  ½ ounce (15 mL) fresh lemon juice

  2 ounces (60 mL) gin

  ½ ounce (15 mL) grenadine (see page 146)

  2 dashes orange bitters

  Brandied cherry (for garnish)

In a sturdy glass or cocktail shaker, muddle the fresh ginger with the lemon juice.
Add the remaining ingredients and ice and shake well. Double strain into a chilled
coupe and serve garnished with a brandied cherry.

  YIELD: 1 COCKTAIL

SATAN'S WHISKERS

¾ OUNCE (23 mL) GIN

¾ OUNCE (23 mL) ORANGE LIQUEUR

¾ OUNCE (23 mL) DRY VERMOUTH

¾ OUNCE (23 mL) SWEET VERMOUTH

¾ OUNCE (23 mL) ORANGE JUICE

1 DASH ANGOSTURA AROMATIC BITTERS

ORANGE PEEL (FOR GARNISH)

Combine the ingredients in a cocktail shaker filled with ice. Shake well. Strain into a chilled coupe and serve garnished with a flamed orange peel.

YIELD: 1 COCKTAIL

SAZERAC

I love anything that reminds me of New Orleans, and this classic has been served there since 1838. Folks get persnickety about how a Sazerac must be made, and some will tell you that it needs a lemon twist while others will tell you it should get the essential oils of the twist but the garnish itself must not be dropped into the drink. I come down on the garnish-free side of this debate. Feel free to add the twist if you prefer; I'm not going to argue as long as you're buying.

¼ OUNCE (8 mL) ABSINTHE (FOR RINSE)

2 OUNCES (60 mL) RYE

½ OUNCE (15 mL) SIMPLE SYRUP

2 DASHES PEYCHAUD'S BITTERS

Pour the absinthe into a chilled rocks glass and swirl the contents to coat the inside of the glass. Discard the excess. Combine the rye, simple syrup, and bitters in a cocktail shaker filled with ice. Stir well. Strain the contents of the cocktail shaker into the cold, absinthe-rinsed rocks glass. Serve up ungarnished.

YIELD: 1 COCKTAIL

SCOFFLAW

During prohibition the Anti-Saloon League launched a contest to create a word to describe "a lawless drinker of illegally made or illegally obtained liquor." The winner received a $200 prize, and Harry's New York Bar in Paris received what was possibly the best cocktail-naming opportunity ever.

1½ OUNCES (45 mL) RYE

1 OUNCE (30 mL) DRY VERMOUTH

¾ OUNCE (23 mL) FRESH LEMON JUICE

¾ OUNCE (23 mL) GRENADINE (SEE PAGE 146)

LEMON TWIST (FOR GARNISH)

Combine the ingredients in a cocktail shaker filled with ice. Shake well. Strain into a chilled coupe and serve garnished with a lemon twist.

YIELD: 1 COCKTAIL

SHERRY COCKTAIL

¾ OUNCE (23 mL) FINO SHERRY

¾ OUNCE (23 mL) OLOROSO SHERRY

½ OUNCE (15 mL) BENEDICTINE

½ OUNCE (15 mL) MARASCHINO LIQUEUR

1 DROP ABSINTHE

ORANGE PEEL (FOR GARNISH)

Combine both sherries, the Benedictine, and the maraschino liqueur in a cocktail shaker filled with ice. Shake well. Strain into a chilled coupe. Finish with the drop of absinthe. Serve garnished with flamed orange peel.

YIELD: 1 COCKTAIL

SIDECAR

GRANULATED SUGAR

1½ OUNCE (45 mL) VS BRANDY

1 OUNCE (30 mL) ORANGE LIQUEUR

¾ OUNCE (23 mL) FRESH LEMON JUICE

Rim a chilled coupe with sugar and set aside. Combine the brandy, orange liqueur, and lemon juice in a cocktail shaker filled with ice. Shake well. Strain into the sugar-rimmed coupe and serve.

YIELD: 1 COCKTAIL

SINGAPORE SLING

1 OUNCE (30 mL) GIN

1 OUNCE (30 mL) CHERRY HEERING

1 OUNCE (30 mL) BENEDICTINE

2 OUNCE (60 mL) PINEAPPLE JUICE

½ OUNCE (15 mL) FRESH LEMON JUICE

½ OUNCE (15 mL) FRESH LIME JUICE

DASH GRENADINE (SEE PAGE 147)

CLUB SODA

PINEAPPLE FLAG (FOR GARNISH)

Combine the ingredients (except for the club soda) in a cocktail shaker filled with ice. Shake well. Empty the entire contents of the cocktail shaker into a tall glass, add additional ice if necessary, and top with club soda. Stir and serve garnished with a fresh pineapple flag.

YIELD: 1 COCKTAIL

SLOE GIN FROZE

The original Waring Blendor cocktail guide took all manner of cocktails and tossed them in a blender to see what would happen. I don't know how they expected the Sloe Gin Fizz to stay frozen once you topped it with club soda, but that's OK, because I never liked the club soda part anyway. This is the only version of a Sloe Gin Fizz I've ever liked…and there's no fizz.

1½ OUNCES (45 mL) SLOE GIN

1 OUNCE (30 mL) GINGER LIQUEUR

½ OUNCE (15 mL) FRESH LEMON JUICE

½ OUNCE (15 mL) SIMPLE SYRUP

1 CUP (237 mL) CRACKED ICE

LEMON WHEEL (FOR GARNISH)

Combine the ingredients in a blender and blend on high until smooth. Pour into a well-chilled glass and serve garnished with a lemon wheel.

YIELD: 1 COCKTAIL

SMOKE ON THE WATER ▾

1¼ OUNCE (38 mL) MEZCAL
¾ OUNCE (23 mL) GINGER LIQUEUR
¼ OUNCE (8 mL) AGAVE SYRUP
½ OUNCE (15 mL) FRESH LEMON JUICE
WATERMELON, SEEDED, 3-INCH CHUNK
JALAPENO (FOR GARNISH)

In a sturdy glass or cocktail shaker, muddle the watermelon with the agave syrup. Add the mezcal, ginger liqueur, lemon juice and ice and shake well. Strain into a double old fashioned glass with ice. Garnish with jalapeno rings slid around a drinking straw.

YIELD: 1 COCKTAIL

SMOKEY MOUNTAIN RICKEY

LIME WEDGE (FOR GARNISH)

2 OUNCES (60 mL) CATDADDY MOONSHINE

½ OUNCE (15 mL) CRANBERRY JUICE

½ OUNCE (15 mL) FRESH LIME JUICE

3-4 OUNCES (90-120 mL) CLUB SODA

Rim a collins glass with the lime wedge. Combine the Catdaddy, cranberry juice, and lime juice in the glass. Add ice, and top with the club soda. Stir gently. Squeeze the lime into the glass, drop it in, and serve.

YIELD: 1 COCKTAIL

SOUR

This makes an unbeatable Whiskey Sour and will become Dan's mother's ruin if I don't stop offering to make them. As my standard sour recipe it allows for some creativity, like pairing vodka with the ginger syrup (see page 146).

2 OUNCES (60 mL) BLENDED WHISKEY, SCOTCH WHISKY, OR VODKA

½ OUNCE (15 mL) FRESH LEMON JUICE

½ OUNCE (15 mL) FRESH LIME JUICE

¾ OUNCE (23 mL) SIMPLE SYRUP

CHERRY FLAG (FOR GARNISH)

Combine the ingredients in a cocktail shaker filled with ice. Shake very well. Strain into a double rocks glass with one large ice chunk. Serve garnished with a cherry flag.

YIELD: 1 COCKTAIL

SOVIET SPRING ⅄

    1 EGG WHITE

    2 OUNCES (60 mL) APRICOT BRANDY

    1 OUNCE (30 mL) FRESH LEMON JUICE

    1 OUNCE (30 mL) FRESH LIME JUICE

    1 OUNCE (30 mL) SIMPLE SYRUP

    3 DROPS ALLSPICE DRAM

Dry shake the egg white (see page 35). Add the apricot brandy, lemon juice, lime juice, simple syrup, and ice and shake vigorously a second time. Strain over ice into a double old fashioned glass. Serve garnished with the 3 drops of allspice dram over the foam.

    YIELD: 1 COCKTAIL

SPICED PISCO SOUR

    1 EGG WHITE

    1½ OUNCES (45 mL) PISCO

    ½ OUNCE (15 mL) TURBINADO SYRUP (SEE PAGE 27)

    ¼ OUNCE (8 mL) CINNAMON SYRUP (SEE PAGE 146)

¼ ounce (8 mL) fresh lemon juice

¼ ounce (8 mL) fresh lime juice

Dash Angostura Aromatic Bitters

Dry shake the egg white (see page 35). Add all the ingredients (except the bitters) and ice to the cocktail shaker and shake vigorously a second time. Strain into a chilled double old fashioned glass. Serve garnished with a colorful dash of bitters over the foam.

YIELD: 1 COCKTAIL

STINGER

2¼ ounces (68 mL) brandy

¾ ounce (23 mL) crème de menthe

Combine the ingredients in a cocktail shaker filled with ice. Shake well. Strain into a chilled coupe and serve ungarnished.

YIELD: 1 COCKTAIL

STONE FENCE

We have a New Year's Day tradition with our neighbors in Michigan. We go house to house for a progressive cocktail party where each host makes finger foods and a craft cocktail. Our friend Bas introduced me to the Stone Fence on a stunning snowy New Year's evening, proving that good neighbors do indeed make strong fences.

2 ounces (60 mL) bourbon

½ ounce (15 mL) fresh lemon juice

¼ ounce (8 mL) ginger syrup (see page 146)

Apple cider

Cinnamon stick (for garnish)

Combine the bourbon, lemon juice, and ginger syrup in a cocktail shaker filled with ice. Shake well. Strain into a double rocks glass filled with ice and top with apple cider. Serve garnished with freshly grated cinnamon.

YIELD: 1 COCKTAIL

STRAWBERRY PIMM'S CUP

Our bartender Kris developed this Pimm's Cup version, and it's hands down one of our guests' favorite cocktails.

> 2 ounces (60 mL) Pimm's No. 1
> 1 ounce (30 mL) Strawberry Cucumber Puree (see page 151)
> 3–4 ounces (90–120 mL) ginger ale
> Lemon wedge (for garnish)

Combine the Pimm's and Strawberry Cucumber Puree in a tall glass filled with ice. Top with the ginger ale. Serve garnished with a lemon wedge.

> *YIELD: 1 COCKTAIL*

TAMARIND PALOMA

> Lime wedge (for garnish)
> 2 ounces (60 mL) silver tequila
> ½ ounce (15 mL) fresh lime juice
> Pinch salt*
> 3–4 ounces (90–120 mL) tamarind soda

Rim a collins glass with the lime wedge. Combine the tequila, lime juice, and salt in the glass. Add ice and top with the tamarind soda. Stir gently. Squeeze the lime into the glass, drop it in and, serve.

* The Paloma is traditionally made with the salt included in the drink as opposed to around the rim of the glass, and this is the preferable method.

> *YIELD: 1 COCKTAIL*

◂ TANG MIMOSA

Admittedly, this is not a pre-Prohibition cocktail. But the history of Tang allows me to toss in this fizzy brunch drink for retro giggles. It's based on the Italian tradition of dropping sugar cubes into a glass of champagne to wish you a sweet life.

> 1 or 2 Tang Cubes (see page 151)
> 1 (750-mL) bottle sparkling wine or prosecco

Add the Tang Cubes to an empty champagne flute. Top with sparkling wine and serve ungarnished.

> *YIELD: 1 COCKTAIL*

TEANI ▲

>   1 OUNCE (30 mL) GREEN TEA-INFUSED APPLEJACK (SEE PAGE 145)
>
>   1 OUNCE (30 mL) APPLE JUICE
>
>   1 OUNCE (30 mL) HONEY SYRUP (SEE PAGE 147)
>
>   BRANDIED CHERRY AND LEMON FLAG (FOR GARNISH)

Combine the ingredients in a cocktail shaker filled with ice. Shake well. Strain into the chilled coupe and serve garnished with the brandied cherry and lemon flag.

>   *YIELD: 1 COCKTAIL*

TEQUILA OLD FASHIONED

I like this drink a tad on the sweet side but cut the agave syrup down, if you prefer.

>   2 OUNCES (60 mL) TEQUILA REPOSADO
>
>   1½ TEASPOONS AGAVE SYRUP
>
>   2 DASHES ANGOSTURA AROMATIC BITTERS
>
>   LEMON TWIST (FOR GARNISH)

Combine the ingredients in a cocktail shaker filled with ice. Stir well. Strain into a double rocks glass with one large ice chunk. Serve garnished with a lemon twist.

>   *YIELD: 1 COCKTAIL*

TEXAS SANGRIA ▾

Is Sangria a vintage drink? It's the oldest, although George Washington would have called it "punch" when he served it at campaign rallies…and, of course, he wouldn't have known about Texas. I originally created this recipe to feature a wine I had brought in from the Lone Star State. I paired it with the spicy jalapeño and tangy tamarind to make it feel at home, and the result is wonderfully Tex-Mex. Serve it up with barbecue.

1 (750-ML) BOTTLE DRY RED WINE

¾ CUP (178 mL) VODKA

¾ CUP (178 mL) JALAPEÑO SYRUP (SEE PAGE 147)

¼ CUP (59 mL) CLOVE TINCTURE (SEE PAGE 144)

1¼ CUP (298 mL) TAMARIND SODA*

JICAMA (FOR GARNISH)

Combine the wine, vodka, jalapeño syrup, and clove tincture in a large pitcher with ice. Stir. Top with the tamarind soda right before serving. Serve over ice in a Texas-sized wine glass, garnished with a long stick of fresh jicama.

*Tamarind soda is available at Latin grocery stores. Look for Jarritos brand.

YIELD: 1 PITCHER

THOMAS AND JEREMIAH

One of the many fun drinks found in Here's How, *my 1941 wood-covered bartender's guide crammed with great old recipes. It's also stuffed with crazy and inappropriate illustrations, like the one for this drink that depicts a line drawing of drunken Thomas (or is it Jeremiah?) passed out under a table.*

¾ OUNCE (23 mL) AMARETTO

¾ OUNCE (23 mL) DEMERARA OR DARK RUM

½ OUNCE (15 mL) TURBINADO SYRUP (SEE PAGE 27)

½ OUNCE (15 mL) FRESH LIME JUICE

3-4 OUNCES (90-120 mL) PEAR CIDER

FRESH PEAR (FOR GARNISH)

Combine the amaretto, rum, turbinado syrup, and lime juice in a tall glass filled with ice. Stir well and top with the pear cider. Serve garnished with a slice of soft, ripe pear.

YIELD: 1 COCKTAIL

TOAST AND JAM

1 OUNCE (30 mL) SCOTCH WHISKY

1 OUNCE (30 mL) SWEET VERMOUTH

½ OUNCE (15 mL) STRAWBERRY BALSAMIC SHRUB (SEE P 149)

¼ OUNCE (8 mL) SIMPLE SYRUP

BRANDIED CHERRY (FOR GARNISH)

Combine the ingredients in a cocktail shaker filled with ice. Shake well. Strain into a chilled coupe and serve garnished with a brandied cherry.

YIELD: 1 COCKTAIL

TODOS VERDE

The Caipirinha is the national drink of Brazil and has been around as long as anyone can remember. This is a Caipirinha with a few of my favorite things.

1 KIWI, PEELED AND CHOPPED

6 LEAVES MINT

½ LIME, QUARTERED

2 TEASPOONS WHITE GRANULATED SUGAR

2 OUNCES (60 mL) CACHAÇA

Muddle the kiwi, mint, and lime with the sugar in a shaker. Add the cachaça and ice. Shake well. Empty the entire contents of the shaker into a double old fashioned glass. Garnish with kiwi and serve.

YIELD: 1 COCKTAIL

TOM AND JERRY

Jerry Thomas is credited with this extremely famous version of eggnog, which at one point was synonymous with Christmas. The procedure requires making a batter to be used as a base for the added hot milk. Versions have been both mass marketed and handcrafted, but in this case I would like to feature one by Audrey Saunders, who got me so excited about cocktails in the first place. It's a bit complicated, but in her words, the extra work is well worth it: "It's so handcrafted. It says everything about the holidays you can't say in words."

12 EGGS

4 CUPS (800 G) GRANULATED SUGAR

3 TABLESPOONS (45 mL) VANILLA EXTRACT

1 (750-mL) BOTTLE DEMERARA OR DARK RUM

4 DASHES ANGOSTURA AROMATIC BITTERS

1 TEASPOON GROUND CINNAMON

½ TEASPOON GROUND CLOVES

¾ TEASPOON GROUND ALLSPICE

½ TEASPOON GROUND NUTMEG

1 (750-mL) BOTTLE BRANDY

WHOLE MILK

WHOLE NUTMEG (FOR GARNISH)

Separate the eggs and place the yolks and whites in separate bowls. Beat the whites until stiff. Add the sugar to the yolks and beat lightly, then add the vanilla, 2 ounces (60 mL) of the rum, the bitters, and the spices. Fold the egg whites into the yolk mixture until it has the consistency of pancake batter. The batter can be kept refrigerated for up to one day.

To serve, pour 1 tablespoon of batter into a warm mug. Add 1 ounce (30 mL) of rum and 1 ounce (30 mL) of brandy to the batter, stirring constantly to avoid curdling. Top with boiling milk and stir until foamy. Serve garnished with freshly grated nutmeg.

YIELD: 24 SERVINGS

TUSCAN 75

1 ounce (30 mL) Fennel-Infused Gin (see page 145)

1 ounce (30 mL) fresh lemon juice

½ ounce (15 mL) simple syrup

Sparkling wine or prosecco

Lemon twist (for garnish)

Combine the gin, lemon juice, and simple syrup in a cocktail shaker filled with ice. Shake well. Strain into a chilled champagne glass and top with sparkling wine. Stir gently and serve garnished with as long and curly a lemon twist as you can muster.

YIELD: 1 COCKTAIL

UNLICENSED SOUR

1½ ounces (45 mL) rye

¾ ounce (23 mL) Catdaddy Moonshine

¾ ounce (23 mL) turbinado syrup (see page 27)

¾ ounce (23 mL) fresh lemon juice

Brandied cherry (for garnish)

Combine the ingredients in a cocktail shaker filled with ice. Shake well. Strain into a double rocks glass filled with ice and serve garnished with a brandied cherry.

YIELD: 1 COCKTAIL

VERMONT COFFEE

I love this drink (big surprise), and it is a feature at our restaurant, where we make it with a maple-infused whiskey. Feel free to either buy a bottle (Cabin Fever is my choice) or infuse one yourself.

1 teaspoon pure maple syrup

8 ounces (240 mL) hot coffee

1½ ounces (45 mL) whiskey

Unsweetened whipped cream

Add the maple syrup to the hot coffee and stir until incorporated. Add the whiskey and top with a healthy dollop of whipped cream.

YIELD: 1 COCKTAIL

THE VESPER

2 ounces (60 mL) gin

1¼ ounces (38 mL) vodka

½ ounce (15 mL) Lillet Blanc

Lemon twist (for garnish)

Combine the ingredients in a cocktail shaker filled with ice. Stir well. Strain into a chilled coupe and serve garnished with a lemon twist.

YIELD: 1 COCKTAIL

VIEUX CARRE

1 ounce (30 mL) rye

1 ounce (30 mL) brandy

1 ounce (30 mL) sweet vermouth

½ ounce (15 mL) Amaro Averna

2 dashes Angostura Aromatic Bitters

2 dashes Peychaud's Bitters

Lemon twist (for garnish)

Combine the ingredients in a cocktail shaker filled with ice. Shake well. Strain into a chilled coupe and serve garnished with a lemon twist.

YIELD: 1 COCKTAIL

WARD 8

Cocktail guru David Wondrich has a brilliant take on how the proper balance in a Ward 8 leaves "absolutely no taste of liquor. In short, this drink lies like a politician."

2 ounces (60 mL) rye

¾ ounce (23 mL) fresh lemon juice

¾ ounce (23 mL) orange juice

½ ounce (15 mL) grenadine (see page 146)

Brandied cherry (for garnish)

Combine the ingredients in a cocktail shaker filled with ice. Shake well. Strain into a chilled coupe and serve with a brandied cherry.

YIELD: 1 COCKTAIL

WEST MIDLANDS

In the '70s, my mom would occasionally host a ladies' luncheon. She would get super fancy and set out canned salmon in a glass dish for sandwiches. I don't remember her serving cocktails (believe it or not, there was hardly ever any alcohol consumed at my house), but this would have been the perfect choice if they had. I regret that I didn't create this Collins sooner so that my 12-year-old self could have offered them a tall, cool one.

1½ ounces (45 mL) oloroso sherry

¾ ounce (23 mL) maraschino liqueur

½ ounce (15 mL) fresh lemon juice

4 ounces (120 mL) club soda

Lemon wheel (for garnish)

Combine the sherry, maraschino liqueur, and lemon juice in a cocktail shaker filled with ice. Shake well. Strain into a collins glass filled with ice, top with the soda, and serve garnished with a lemon wheel.

YIELD: 1 COCKTAIL

WHISKEY DAISY

1½ ounces (45 mL) rye

½ ounce (15 mL) Yellow Chartreuse

½ ounce (15 mL) fresh lemon juice

¼ ounce (8 mL) fresh lime juice

½ ounce (15 mL) turbinado syrup (see page 27)

2–3 ounces (60–90 mL) club soda

Fresh mint (for garnish)

Combine the rye, chartreuse, lemon and lime juices, and turbinado syrup in a cocktail shaker filled with ice. Shake well. Strain into a collins glass filled with crushed ice and top with the club soda. Stir and serve garnished with fresh mint.

YIELD: 1 COCKTAIL

WHITE LADY

Harry Craddock includes this recipe in The Savoy Cocktail Book. *A few others lay claim to this drink, essentially a sidecar with gin in place of brandy, but the others can't say that they used to serve it regularly to Laurel and Hardy. So, point Craddock.*

> 1½ ounces (45 mL) gin
>
> 1 ounce (30 mL) orange liqueur
>
> 1 ounce (30 mL) fresh lemon juice
>
> Lemon wheel, thinly sliced (for garnish)

Combine the ingredients in a cocktail shaker filled with ice. Shake well. Strain into a chilled coupe and serve garnished with a floating lemon wheel.

YIELD: 1 COCKTAIL

WIDOW'S KISS ▲

I insist you make this with French apple brandy (Calvados), which is more delicate but complex than others. When done right, you'll find this vintage cocktail is aptly named.

> 1½ ounces (45 mL) Calvados
>
> ¾ ounce (23 mL) Yellow Chartreuse
>
> ¾ ounce (23 mL) Benedictine
>
> 2 dashes Angostura Aromatic Bitters
>
> Maraschino cherry (for garnish)

Combine the ingredients in a cocktail shaker filled with ice. Shake well. Strain into a chilled coupe and serve garnished with a maraschino cherry.

> *YIELD: 1 COCKTAIL*

WOMAN OF FASHION

This is a riff on a cocktail I uncovered in So Red the Nose, a dusty estate sale find filled with cocktail submissions from the literati of 1935. Poet Marion Strobel offered it up alongside this pithy quote: "This will make three cocktails and will probably dispose of the weakest member of the triangle."

> 1½ ounces (45 mL) bourbon
>
> 1 ounce (30 mL) applejack
>
> ½ ounce (15 mL) fresh orange juice
>
> ¼ ounce (8 mL) fresh lime juice
>
> ¼ ounce (8 mL) simple syrup

> *YIELD: 1 COCKTAIL (I CAN'T BELIEVE MARION WOULD DIVIDE THIS BY 3!)*

YELLOW BIRD

2 ounces (60 mL) Demerara or dark rum

½ ounce (15 mL) Galliano

½ ounce (15 mL) orange liqueur

½ ounce (15 mL) fresh lime juice

Lime wheel, thinly sliced (for garnish)

Combine the ingredients in a cocktail shaker filled with ice. Shake well. Strain into a chilled coupe and serve garnished with a floating lime wheel.

YIELD: 1 COCKTAIL

YVETTE AND CRÈME ▿

1½ ounces (45 mL) Old Tom Gin

1 ounce (30 mL) Crème Yvette

¾ ounce (23 mL) half-and-half

Nasturtiums or other edible flowers (for garnish)

Combine the ingredients in a double rocks glass filled with ice. Stir well and serve garnished with an edible nasturtium.

YIELD: 1 COCKTAIL

SUB-RECIPES

Infusions

BACON-INFUSED BOURBON

> 1 (750-ML) BOTTLE BOURBON
>
> 10 STRIPS THICK-CUT BACON
>
> 1 MEDIUM CINNAMON STICK, BROKEN INTO PIECES

1. Preheat the oven to 300°F (150°C).

2. Lay the bacon flat on a baking sheet and place it in the oven. Bake until crisp but not brittle. Remove from the oven and let cool 5 minutes. Transfer the bacon to a paper towel–lined plate, reserving the fat. Save the bacon for another use.

3. Transfer the bourbon to a clean jar with a tight-fitting lid, reserving the empty bottle. Add the bacon fat and cinnamon stick and seal the jar. Store in a dark, cool place for five days, gently shaking the jar daily. Transfer the jar to the freezer on day five and allow the infusion to separate. Remove it from the freezer once the bacon fat has risen to the top and become firm. Discard the solidified fat and strain the infused bourbon through a cheesecloth. Repeat the straining process three additional times, each time with fresh cheesecloth or a coffee filter. Return the infused bourbon to its original bottle and store until ready to use.

> *YIELD: 1 (750-mL) BOTTLE*

CLOVE TINCTURE

> ½ CUP (119 mL) SILVER TEQUILA
>
> 20–30 WHOLE CLOVES

Place the ingredients in a clean jar with a tight-fitting lid. Seal tightly and let the cloves steep for 6 to 8 hours, gently shaking the jar occasionally. Do not leave the cloves in the tincture too long, as they intensify and become overpowering fairly quickly. Strain, discarding the cloves, and store until ready to use.

> *YIELD: ½ CUP (119 mL)*

FENNEL-INFUSED GIN

1 FENNEL BULB, CUT AND QUARTERED, FRONDS RESERVED

1 (750-ML) BOTTLE GIN

1. Place the fennel bulbs in a clean jar with a tight-fitting lid. Gently crush the fennel fronds to release their flavor and add them to the jar. Loosely fill the jar to capacity without overcrowding. Pour the gin over the fennel, reserving the empty gin bottle.

2. Seal tightly and store in a dark, cool place for at least four days, gently shaking the jar daily. Begin tasting on day four, and let the infusion continue until the taste is to your liking or the fennel fronds begin to dull and lose their bright color. Strain to remove the solids and store the infused gin in the original bottle.

YIELD: 1 (750-mL) BOTTLE

GREEN TEA–INFUSED APPLEJACK

1 (750-ML) BOTTLE APPLEJACK

6 TABLESPOONS (66 G) LOOSE GREEN TEA

1. Transfer the applejack to a clean jar with a tight-fitting lid, reserving the empty bottle. Add the green tea and seal the jar.

2. Let the tea steep for approximately 60 to 90 minutes, gently shaking the jar occasionally. Begin tasting after 60 minutes and let the infusion continue until the taste is to your liking; a longer infusion will result in a more intense tea flavor. Strain to remove the solids and store the applejack in the original bottle.

YIELD: 1 (750-mL) BOTTLE

HORSERADISH-INFUSED VODKA

1 (750-ML) BOTTLE VODKA

1 (4-INCH [10-CM]) PIECE HORSERADISH ROOT, PEELED

1. Cut the horseradish root into approximately 8 pieces, about ½ inch (13 mm) each. Place the pieces in a clean jar with a tight-fitting lid. Pour the vodka over the horseradish, reserving the empty bottle.

2. Seal tightly and store in a dark, cool place for at least one week and up to a month, gently shaking the jar daily. Begin tasting on day seven and let the infusion continue until the taste is to your liking. This infusion can be left up to a month. Strain to remove the solids and store it in the original bottle.

YIELD: 1 (750-mL) BOTTLE

Syrups

CINNAMON SYRUP

1 CUP (237 mL) WATER

1 CUP (200 G) GRANULATED SUGAR

6 MEDIUM CINNAMON STICKS, BROKEN INTO PIECES

Combine the cinnamon, water, and sugar in a saucepan and place it over high heat. Bring to a boil and stir to dissolve the sugar. Lower the heat to medium and simmer until the syrup is reduced to 1 cup (237 mL), about 8 to 10 minutes. Remove from the heat, allow to cool, and let stand for four hours. Strain, discarding the cinnamon, and store in the refrigerator for up to 2 weeks.

YIELD: 1 CUP (237 mL)

GINGER SYRUP

1 (3-INCH [7.5-CM]) PIECE FRESH GINGER

1 CUP (237 mL) WATER

1 CUP (200 G) GRANULATED SUGAR

Peel the ginger and cut it into about 6 equal pieces. Combine the ginger, water, and sugar in a saucepan and place it over high heat. Bring to a boil and stir to dissolve the sugar. Lower the heat to medium and simmer until the syrup is reduced to 1 cup (237 mL), about 8 to 10 minutes. Remove from the heat and let cool. Strain, discarding the ginger, and store in the refrigerator for up to 2 weeks.

YIELD: 1 CUP (237 mL)

GRENADINE

2 CUPS (474 mL) 100% PURE POMEGRANATE JUICE

2 CUPS (400 G) RAW SUGAR

1 TEASPOON ORANGE BLOSSOM WATER

Combine the pomegranate juice and sugar in a saucepan and place it over medium heat. Bring to a simmer and stir to dissolve the sugar. Simmer until the mixture is reduced to 1½ cups (356 mL), about 8 to 10 minutes. Remove from the heat, stir in the orange blossom water, and let cool. Store in the refrigerator for up to 2 weeks.*

Optionally, 1 ounce (30 mL) of vodka can be added as preservative.

YIELD: 1½ CUPS (356 mL)

HONEY SYRUP

¼ CUP (59 mL) WATER

¾ CUP (178 mL) HONEY

Combine the water and honey in a saucepan and place it over high heat. Bring to a boil and stir until fully incorporated. Remove from the heat and allow to cool. Store in the refrigerator until ready to use.

YIELD: 1 CUP (237 mL)

JALAPEÑO SYRUP

2 WHOLE FRESH JALAPEÑOS

1 CUP (237 mL) WATER

2 CUPS (400 G) GRANULATED SUGAR

Halve the jalapeños lengthwise and discard the seeds and inner membranes. Slice the halves lengthwise into 4 to 6 long strips.

Combine the jalapeños, water, and sugar in a saucepan and place it over high heat. Bring to a boil and stir to dissolve the sugar. Lower the heat to medium and simmer until the syrup is reduced to 1 cup (237 mL), about 8 to 10 minutes. Remove from the heat, allow to cool, and let stand for four hours. Strain, discarding the jalapeños, and store in the refrigerator for up to 2 weeks.

YIELD: 1 CUP (237 mL)

LAVENDER SYRUP

1 CUP (237 mL) WATER

1 TABLESPOON DRIED LAVENDER FLOWERS

½ CUP (100 G) GRANULATED SUGAR

1 CUP (237 mL) HONEY

In a saucepan, bring the water and lavender flowers to a boil. Add the sugar and honey and bring to a second boil, stirring to dissolve the sugar. Lower the heat to medium and simmer for 5 minutes. Remove from the heat and allow to cool. Strain, discarding the lavender flowers, and store in the refrigerator for up to 2 weeks.

YIELD: 1 CUP (237 mL)

ORGEAT SYRUP

I've been thinking a lot about orgeat syrup (pronounced oôr-zhä) …because that's what I do. It's the "wow" factor in the best tiki drinks. Nothing else has the consistency and flavor of this almond-based syrup, and I was all set to tell you how to make your own. But I've changed my mind. It's a whole process of roasting almonds and removing the skins before adding almond flour and both rose water and orange water—or you could buy a bottle for $3.99. There just isn't enough difference in flavor to warrant this much work, unless you were really trying to prove a point. So, here's the deal: I give you a pass on the homemade orgeat syrup thing, and you spend an extra hour doing homework with your kids…or dusting the living room…or playing golf. Or better yet, take the time you saved to enjoy a fabulous cocktail, and raise a glass to me.

PINEAPPLE SYRUP

1 cup (237 mL) water

1 cup (200 g) granulated sugar

1 cup cubed fresh pineapple (approximately 1-inch [2.5-cm] cubes)

Combine the water and sugar in a saucepan and place it over high heat. Bring to a boil and stir to dissolve the sugar. Add the pineapple and bring to a second boil. Lower the heat to medium and simmer for 8 to 10 minutes, gently pressing on the pineapple occasionally with a spoon to help release the juices. Remove from the heat and allow to cool. Store in the refrigerator for up to 2 weeks.

YIELD: 1½ CUPS (356 ML)

ROSEMARY SYRUP

4 sprigs fresh rosemary

2 cups (474 mL) water

1 cup (200 g) granulated sugar

Squeeze the rosemary to bruise it and release the oils. Combine the rosemary, water, and sugar in a saucepan and place it over high heat. Bring to a boil and stir until the sugar is dissolved. Reduce the heat and simmer for about 8 to 10 minutes. Remove from the heat and allow to cool. Strain, discarding the rosemary, and store in the refrigerator for up to 2 weeks.

YIELD: 1½ CUPS (356 mL)

Note: Mint Syrup can be made by substituting a small bunch (about 20 leaves) of mint for the rosemary.

Shrubs

SHRUBS WERE POPULAR IN COLONIAL AMERICA AS A WAY TO CONSERVE summer fruits and juices into the year. Basically, they are made by adding acid, often in the form of vinegar, as a preservative. A shrub could be mixed with water for summer coolers or set aside and aged as a punch base (as Ben Franklin did). My passion for homemade shrubs is based on the surprising tang you get from adding vinegar to a cocktail; plus, they're fun to make.

RASPBERRY SHRUB

1 CUP (200 G) GRANULATED SUGAR

1 CUP (237 ML) WATER

1 PINT (246 G) FRESH RASPBERRIES

1 CUP (237 ML) CHAMPAGNE VINEGAR

Combine the sugar and water in a saucepan and place it over high heat. Bring to a boil and stir to dissolve the sugar. Add the raspberries, reduce the heat to medium, and simmer for 8 to 10 minutes. Add the vinegar and simmer for 10 additional minutes. Remove from the heat and allow to cool. Strain to remove the solids and store in the refrigerator until ready to use.

YIELD: APPROXIMATELY 2 CUPS (474 mL)

STRAWBERRY BALSAMIC SHRUB

1 CUP (200 G) GRANULATED SUGAR

1 CUP (237 ML) WATER

1 POUND (454 G) FRESH STRAWBERRIES, HULLED AND HALVED

1 TABLESPOON WHOLE BLACK PEPPERCORNS, CRACKED

½ CUP (119 ML) GOOD-QUALITY BALSAMIC VINEGAR

Combine the sugar and water in a saucepan and place it over high heat. Bring to a boil and stir to dissolve the sugar. Add the strawberries and black pepper, reduce the heat to medium, and simmer for 8 to10 minutes. Add the balsamic vinegar and simmer for 10 additional minutes. Remove from the heat and allow to cool. Strain to remove the solids and store in the refrigerator until ready to use.

YIELD: APPROXIMATELY 2 CUPS (474 mL)

Garnishes

BRANDIED CHERRIES ▼

    1 POUND (454 G) FRESH BLACK CHERRIES, PITTED

    1 CUP (237 mL) BRANDY

    1 TEASPOON CORIANDER

    1 TEASPOON WHOLE CLOVES

    2 CINNAMON STICKS, BROKEN

    4 TABLESPOONS (50 G) DEMERARA SUGAR

Combine all the ingredients in a saucepan and place it over medium heat. Be careful not to boil, as this will burn off the alcohol. Bring to a low simmer and cook for approximately 10 minutes. Remove from the heat, allow to cool, and strain, reserving the juice. Store the brandied cherries and their juice in the refrigerator.

YIELD: 1 POUND (454 G)

ROASTED PEAR PUREE

2 FRESH PEARS

1 TABLESPOON HONEY

Preheat the oven to 375°F (190°C). Arrange two pieces of aluminum foil on a flat surface and place one pear in the center of each. Drizzle both with the honey and loosely wrap them in the foil, leaving the tops open. Place the pears in the top half of the oven and roast until they are buttery soft, about 50 to 60 minutes. Remove them from the oven and let them cool. Peel the skins off with your hands and pull the flesh away from the core. Place the peeled pears in a blender with any accumulated juices and puree until smooth. Pour into a container and store in the refrigerator for up to 1 week.

YIELD: ¾ CUP (178 mL)

STRAWBERRY CUCUMBER PUREE

1 OUNCE (30 mL) GIN (AS PRESERVATIVE)

1 PINT (332 G) STRAWBERRIES, HULLED AND QUARTERED

1 CUCUMBER, PEELED

6 OUNCES (180 mL) FRESH LEMON JUICE

1 TABLESPOON GRANULATED SUGAR

In a food processor fitted with the metal blade, combine all the ingredients. Process to a smooth puree, about 30 seconds. Store in the refrigerator for up to 2 weeks.

YIELD: ¾ CUP (178 mL)

TANG CUBES

2 CUPS (400 G) TANG

2 TEASPOONS WATER

Using a food processor, mix the ingredients to a "wet sand" consistency. Press the mixture into a 5 x 8-inch (12.5 x 20-cm) pan. Place a second 5 x 8-inch (12.5 x 20-cm) pan on top of the Tang mixture and press forcefully to compress. Flip the pans, remove the top pan, and let the mixture air dry for 40 minutes. Score the Tang into 1–inch (2.5-cm) square cubes, making sure not to cut all the way through. Let the cubes dry another 30 minutes before cutting through the scored lines. Air dry the cubes overnight. Store in an airtight container; do not refrigerate.

SNACKS

I REMEMBER STOPPING WITH FRIENDS AT A LONG ISLAND BAR DURING that awkward interim between a wedding ceremony and reception. It was a random smoke-filled dive serviced by a middle-aged bartender in a not-so-clean shirt. Down at the end of the bar sat one lone guy nursing something on the rocks, and in front of him sat the only free food between now and the cocktail hour: a plastic bowl of goldfish crackers. More broke than proud, we called down to our new pal, "Hey! How about some of those fish?"

This chapter glorifies the bar snack—that small bite that packs a large punch of flavor. The pickled snap that makes you yearn for an icy cocktail in a swanky glass. The bowl of salty crunch designed to create just the right bit of parch on the tongue. These recipes are simple to serve and easy to eat while clasping a chilled coupe. That's what I want to find at the end of my bar and, in a (pun intended) nutshell, that's my bar snack philosophy.

Dan Smith

Deep-Fried Snacks

WE ALL KNOW THE DRAWBACKS TO DEEP-FRIED FOODS…AND WE ALL know how tasty they are, especially with an adult beverage. This being acknowledged, there are several steps to be taken to minimize the health drawbacks and maximize the pleasure, so here goes:

✦ USE GOOD-QUALITY COOKING OIL.

Use one with a high smoke point (which just means that you can heat it to a higher temperature without it breaking down). My choices are sunflower and safflower oils—they're higher in unsaturated fats, so they're generally looked upon as healthier for the old ticker.

✦ INVEST IN A COUNTERTOP DEEP FRYER.

I know many people would rather turn in their "foodie" card than purchase one of these, but let's look at the benefits. They're self-contained, they're equipped with an internal thermometer, they often have a built-in timer, they always have a cover, and they're relatively inexpensive. Alternatively, you can use a deep pot on your stovetop—just make sure that you have a deep-fry thermometer.

✦ CONTROL THE TEMPERATURE.

All of the recipes in this section have been created with an oil temperature of 350°F (180°C) in mind. If you have a countertop fryer, just set it and forget it. It'll do the rest of the work for you, and that includes kicking back in when the temperature drops. If you're using a deep-fry thermometer, clip it to the side of the pot and let it come to 350°F (180°C). Keep in mind that you'll have to fiddle with the heat to keep it steadily at the correct temperature. If you don't have a deep-fry thermometer, use the bread cube method. Drop a 1-inch (2.5-cm) cube of white bread into the hot oil—if it browns in sixty seconds, you're good to go. For inexperienced cooks, this is the least desirable method.

✦ TRIPLE DIP.

No, it's not that disgusting habit some people have of sticking their half-eaten chips into bowls of dip meant for people other than themselves. It's the method of coating food first in flour, then egg, then some type of crunchy coating. I use it often in this section, so it's worth noting that the process is always the same. It's also worth noting that you'll benefit from taking the time to chill the food after it's been breaded. Chilling helps the coating stick when it's dropped into the hot oil.

✦ IN ALL THINGS, MODERATION.

If you eat nothing but deep-fried food, you can expect the bad health that goes along with this diet. If you enjoy it on occasion, then do just that…enjoy it!

CHORIZO-CHEDDAR-STUFFED OLIVES ➤

When I first tested this recipe I used Spanish green olives, but I thought the strong flavors of the olives and the chorizo fought with each other. I chose to go with canned black mission olives…the kind my son likes to fit onto each of his ten fingers and then eat off one at a time! They have a milder (some may say boring) flavor, but I think it pairs well with spicy chorizo.

OIL FOR DEEP FRYING

½ CUP (61 G) ALL-PURPOSE FLOUR

¼ TEASPOON SALT

¼ TEASPOON BLACK PEPPER

1 CAN COLOSSAL PITTED MISSION OLIVES

1 EGG, BEATEN

1 TABLESPOON WATER

½ CUP (75 G) SEASONED BREADCRUMBS

2 OUNCES (57 G) MEXICAN CHORIZO*

1 OUNCE (28 G) SHREDDED SHARP CHEDDAR CHEESE

1. Prepare the oil according to the directions at the beginning of this section.

2. In a small bowl, season the flour with the salt and pepper. In a second bowl, whisk together the eggs and water. Place the breadcrumbs in a third bowl.

3. With your hands, mix together the chorizo and cheese. Pull off small pieces and roll them into logs that will fit into the olive holes. Don't be afraid to overstuff the olives—an extra piece of chorizo peeking out of the olive looks good and is tasty.

4. Roll the olives first in the flour, then the egg wash, then the breadcrumbs. Place them on a sheet pan and refrigerate for at least 15 minutes to help the breadcrumbs adhere.

5. Slide the olives into the hot oil and fry for 3 minutes. Remove them from the oil and place them on a paper towel–lined plate. Serve warm. Refrigerate any leftover olives.

YIELD: APPROXIMATELY 16 OLIVES

*Make sure to get Mexican chorizo, not Spanish. Mexican is packed in long, clear tubes and is soft to the touch—sort of like uncooked breakfast sausage meat. Spanish chorizo is more like pepperoni in consistency.

DILL PICKLE CHIPS

Fried pickles are all the rage at the moment. Talk to Southerners, though, and they'll shrug and ask what's the big deal...they've been eating them since Fatman Austin popularized them down in Atkins, Arkansas in 1963.

Make sure to use panko as your breading for these—it's much crunchier than other varieties of breadcrumbs, and I find that it holds up better to the pickle.

OIL FOR DEEP FRYING

2 DOZEN DILL PICKLE CHIPS

1 CUP (121 G) ALL-PURPOSE FLOUR

½ TEASPOON SALT

½ TEASPOON BLACK PEPPER

2 EGGS, BEATEN

2 TABLESPOONS WATER

1 CUP (150 G) PANKO BREADCRUMBS

BUTTERMILK RANCH DIP (RECIPE FOLLOWS)

1. Prepare the oil according to the directions at the beginning of this section.

2. In a small bowl, season the flour with the salt and pepper. In a separate small bowl, whisk the eggs and water together. Place the panko in a third bowl.

3. One at a time, dredge the pickle chips in first the flour, then the egg wash, then the panko. (The pickle chips may be frozen at this point and fried from frozen.)

(continued on next page)

4. Slide the pickle chips into the hot oil a few at a time and fry for 2 to 3 minutes, until the panko is a deep golden brown. Remove from the oil and place on a paper towel–lined plate. Serve warm, with Buttermilk Ranch Dip on the side. These don't hold well, so discard any leftovers.

YIELD: 24 PICKLE CHIPS

BUTTERMILK RANCH DIP

½ CUP (119 mL) GOOD-QUALITY MAYONNAISE

½ CUP (119 mL) SOUR CREAM

½ CUP (119 mL) BUTTERMILK

1 TEASPOON GARLIC POWDER

1 TEASPOON ONION POWDER

½ TEASPOON SMOKED PAPRIKA

½ TEASPOON DRIED DILL

½ TEASPOON DRIED BASIL

½ TEASPOON SALT

½ TEASPOON FRESHLY GROUND BLACK PEPPER

Combine all the ingredients in a bowl and mix well. Refrigerate until ready to use.

FENNEL ONION STRINGS

I don't know anyone who doesn't like fried onions, and that's why I've included a recipe for them. The fennel adds a nice surprise to an old favorite.

1 LARGE SPANISH ONION

2 CUPS (474 mL) BUTTERMILK

1 TABLESPOON GRANULATED SUGAR

OIL FOR DEEP FRYING

1½ CUPS (182 g) ALL-PURPOSE FLOUR

2 TEASPOONS SALT

1 TEASPOON FRESHLY GROUND BLACK PEPPER

FENNEL SALT

1 TABLESPOON FINE SEA SALT

1 TABLESPOON GROUND FENNEL

1. Peel and halve the onion. Thinly slice each half lengthwise, from root end to top. You should have about 4 cups (600 g) total. Pour the buttermilk into a large nonreactive bowl, add the sugar and onions, and toss well. Soak for at least one hour and up to one day.

2. Prepare the oil according to the directions at the beginning of this section.

3. Place the flour in a large mixing bowl and season with the salt and pepper. Drain the onions and dredge them in the flour by the handful. Shake off any excess flour (I use a hand strainer for this—put them in the strainer and shake the excess flour back into the bowl).

4. Slide the onions into the hot oil and fry for 7 minutes, or until they turn a deep golden brown. The onion itself should be crisp, with very little moisture left. Too much moisture will make the onion strings soggy as they sit.

5. Drain the onions on a paper towel–lined plate and sprinkle with a little of the Fennel Salt. Repeat the process with all of the onions, making sure to change the paper towel frequently to absorb the grease. These will keep in an airtight container for several days. Do not refrigerate!

YIELD: APPROXIMATELY 4 CUPS (600 G)

ROSEMARY AND SEA SALT FRIED CHICKPEAS

This is a simple snack that can become addictive. There's almost no prep, and they take less than ten minutes to fry. The perfect recipe for that lonely can of chickpeas that's been sitting in the back of your cabinet for a year.

OIL FOR DEEP FRYING

1 (29-OUNCE [822-G]) CAN CHICKPEAS

1 TABLESPOON FRESH ROSEMARY, FINELY CHOPPED

1 TEASPOON FINELY GROUND SEA SALT

1. Prepare the oil according to the directions at the beginning of this section.

2. Drain the chickpeas and spread them on a paper towel. Blot them with additional paper towels. The drier the chickpeas are, the better; if they're too wet, the oil will spatter and possibly even foam over the lip of the pot.

3. Carefully slide the chickpeas into the oil and fry for 8 to 9 minutes. They will be a deep golden color and should have very little moisture left in them. Drain and immediately toss with the rosemary and sea salt. Let cool and serve. Store in an airtight container for up to 1 week.

YIELD: APPROXIMATELY 3 CUPS (492 G)

REUBEN BALLS ➤

The flavor combo in a Reuben is one of my favorites—salty corned beef, nutty Swiss, sharp sauerkraut, sweet dressing. The idea of putting all that into a bite-sized snack is fabulous…and I'm thankful to one of my team, Paul Wacker, for bringing it to my attention.

1 CUP (121 G) ALL-PURPOSE FLOUR

3 EGGS, BEATEN

3 TABLESPOONS (45 ML) WATER

1 CUP (150 G) SEASONED BREADCRUMBS

1 TEASPOON GROUND CARAWAY SEEDS

6 OUNCES (170 G) CORNED BEEF, MINCED

4 OUNCES (114 G) SWISS CHEESE, SHREDDED

2 OUNCES (57 G) SAUERKRAUT, DRAINED

½ CUP (119 ML) THOUSAND ISLAND DRESSING

2 TEASPOONS KOSHER SALT

1 TEASPOON BLACK PEPPER

OIL FOR DEEP FRYING

1. Place the flour in a small bowl. In a second bowl, whisk together the eggs and water. In a third bowl, combine the breadcrumbs and ground caraway seeds.

2. In a medium bowl, combine the corned beef, Swiss cheese, sauerkraut, dressing, salt, and pepper. Divide this mixture into 24 equal portions and roll each into a ball. One at a time, roll the balls first in the flour, then the egg wash, then the breadrumbs. Place them on a baking sheet and chill for at least 15 minutes to help the breadcrumbs adhere.

3. Prepare the oil according to the directions at the beginning of this section.

4. Slide the balls into the hot oil, making sure not to overcrowd. Fry for 2 to 3 minutes, until they are golden brown. Remove them from the oil and place them on a paper towel–lined plate. Serve warm, or let cool and store in the refrigerator for up to 3 days. Reheat in a 350°F (180°C) oven for 12 to 15 minutes.

YIELD: 24 REUBEN BALLS

SCOTCH QUAIL EGGS

Scotch eggs have been a favorite of mine since the first time I visited England…savory pork sausage wrapped around a hard-boiled egg, and the whole thing deep fried. The conventional chicken's egg tends to be more of a meal, though…it's huge. That's why I thought of using quail eggs. Once they're wrapped in the sausage, the whole package tends to be just a shade smaller than a small chicken egg—perfect for a bar snack. Quail eggs can be found two ways: either fresh or canned in light salt water brine. I would usually advise going with fresh, but the membrane on a quail egg is thicker than one on a chicken egg, which makes peeling them a pain. Go with the canned if it's available to you. Once it's wrapped in sausage meat, breaded, and fried, no one will know anyway.

1 CUP (121 G) ALL-PURPOSE FLOUR

½ TEASPOON SALT

½ TEASPOON BLACK PEPPER

2 EGGS, BEATEN

2 TABLESPOONS WATER

1 CUP (150 G) PANKO BREADCRUMBS

1 POUND (454 G) SEASONED BREAKFAST SAUSAGE MEAT

16 QUAIL EGGS, HARD-BOILED AND PEELED

OIL FOR DEEP FRYING

1. In a small bowl, season the flour with the salt and pepper. In a second bowl, whisk together the eggs and water. Place the panko in a third bowl.

2. Divide the sausage meat into 16 equal portions and shape each portion into a thin patty. Place an egg in the center of a patty and bring the edges of the patty up over the egg. Press well to seal the egg in the sausage meat. Repeat with the remaining eggs. Make sure that they all have a uniform appearance.

3. One at a time, roll the eggs in first the flour, then the egg wash, then the panko. Place them on a cookie sheet and chill for at least 15 minutes to help the panko adhere.

4. Prepare the cooking oil according to the directions at the beginning of this section. Slide the eggs into the hot oil, making sure not to crowd them. You may have to fry them in several batches.

5. Fry for 4 minutes, until the eggs are a deep golden brown. The sausage must be fully cooked through.

6. Remove from the oil and place on a paper towel–lined plate. Scotch eggs can be served warm or at room temperature. Refrigerate any leftover eggs.

YIELD: 16 EGGS

Crispy Snacks

THE ELEMENTS IN THIS SECTION ARE WHAT I THINK OF AS THE LINCHPINS of bar snacks…crispiness, crunchiness, and saltiness. It's no mistake that bars the world over serve up snacks like these in little bowls…not only to create goodwill with the patron, but also to create a powerful thirst that can only be quenched with the former's libations.

You'll find these recipes to be the simplest, fastest, and cleanest of those I've included. Choose a couple as your go-to favorites.

BACON AND CASHEW BRITTLE

Brittle is traditionally more of a dessert. Add bacon and salt, and you've just created a bar-worthy snack. One essential tool you'll need for this recipe is a candy thermometer. If you don't already have one, do yourself a favor and buy one. It comes in handy, and I use mine more than I can tell you.

> 1½ CUPS (300 G) GRANULATED SUGAR
>
> ⅔ CUP (158 ML) PLUS 1½ TEASPOONS WATER, DIVIDED
>
> ⅔ CUP (158 ML) LIGHT CORN SYRUP
>
> 2 TABLESPOONS BUTTER
>
> ¾ CUP (104 G) ROASTED CASHEWS
>
> ¾ CUP (104 G) COOKED AND FINELY CHOPPED BACON
>
> ½ TEASPOON KOSHER SALT
>
> ½ TEASPOON VANILLA EXTRACT
>
> ½ TEASPOON BAKING SODA
>
> 1½ TABLESPOONS COARSE KOSHER SALT (FOR TOPPING)

1. Generously butter a 12 x 18-inch (30 x 45-cm) baking sheet.

2. In a heavy saucepan, mix together the sugar, the ⅔ cup (158 mL) water, and the corn syrup and place over high heat. Stir frequently until the mixture comes to a boil. Clip a candy thermometer to the side of the pan and lower the heat a bit. Continue to boil until the candy thermometer reaches the hard ball stage (250°F [120°C]).

3. Stir in the butter, cashews, and bacon. Continue cooking until the mixture turns a light brown color. Remove from the heat.

4. Mix together the salt, vanilla, baking soda, and remaining 1½ teaspoons water in a small bowl and quickly stir this into the nut mixture.

(continued on next page)

5. Pour the nut mixture onto the baking sheet and use the back of a buttered wooden spoon to spread it thinly and evenly. Sprinkle the top evenly with the kosher salt.

6. Allow the brittle to cool, then break it into pieces. Store in an airtight container in a cool, dry place for up to three weeks.

YIELD: 1 (12 X 18-INCH [30 X 45-CM]) PAN

BACON CORN NUTS

Giant white corn kernels are part of the maize family, as is the sweet corn that we all enjoy in the summertime. In the United States, we're not terribly familiar with white corn, but it's a staple in the Mexican diet, especially when it's treated with an alkali and turned into hominy.

I find dried giant white corn in bodegas (stores specializing in Latino groceries). I've also found it online. It's worth looking for, as it's really versatile, keeps a long time (since it's dried), and makes a great and interesting addition to your pantry. This recipe is based on the Peruvian bar snack, cancha. Munch on some with a Chilcano de Pisco (see page 66).

4 CUPS (640 G) SOAKED GIANT WHITE CORN

¾ POUND (341 G) BACON*

¼ CUP (59 mL) SUNFLOWER OIL

2 TEASPOONS SUGAR

1 TEASPOON CRUSHED RED PEPPER

2 TEASPOONS KOSHER SALT, DIVIDED

2 TEASPOONS ORANGE ZEST

1. Soak the corn for 2 to 3 days. When ready to use, drain and set aside.

2. Preheat the oven to 350°F (180°C).

3. If using bulk bacon, cut into a ½-inch (13-mm) dice and place in a cold skillet. Place the skillet over high heat and cook until the bacon starts to render its fat. Reduce the heat to medium and continue to cook until the bacon becomes just the slightest bit crisp. Add the corn, oil, sugar, red pepper, and 1 teaspoon of the salt. Stir to coat the corn.

4. Spread the corn-bacon mixture evenly onto a 12 x 18-inch (30 x 45-cm) baking sheet and place it in the center of the oven. Bake for 45 to 50 minutes, stirring every 15 minutes to make sure the kernels on the edges don't burn. Test for doneness by biting down on a corn kernel. It shouldn't be chewy at all—it should almost shatter when you bite it.

5. Remove the mixture from the oven and transfer it to a large, paper towel–lined plate to absorb any excess oil. Sprinkle the mix with the remaining salt and the orange zest and toss. Serve at room temperature. Store in an airtight container in a cool, dry place.

YIELD: APPROXIMATELY 5 CUPS (800 G)

*Best-case scenario is a piece of good-quality bulk (meaning unsliced) bacon that has a good amount of fat on it. Next best is good-quality thick-sliced bacon. Don't get thinly sliced bacon for this recipe, and don't go cheap on it, either—inexpensive bacons tend to have a lesser flavor.

CHILI LIME PEPITAS

Pumpkin seeds make a great snack, with or without a cocktail. They're extremely versatile (I've eaten them with yogurt at breakfast, snacked on them at lunch, and candied them for a dessert topping) and they have the added bonus of being nutritious. Roasting them with chili powder and lime makes them a fantastic bar snack.

4 CUPS (424 G) SHELLED RAW PUMPKIN SEEDS

1 TABLESPOON CHILI POWDER

2 TEASPOONS SALT

ZEST OF 3 LIMES

JUICE OF 2 LIMES

¼ CUP (59 ML) SUNFLOWER OIL

1. Preheat the oven to 375°F (190°C).

2. In a large bowl, toss all the ingredients together until the seeds are well coated. Spread the mixture evenly onto a 12 x 18-inch (30 x 45-cm) baking sheet and bake for 20 to 25 minutes. Shake the pan once while baking so that the seeds around the edges don't burn. The seeds will change in color from green to a deep golden brown. Remove and let cool before serving. Store in an airtight container in a cool, dry place.

YIELD: 4 CUPS (424 G)

CRACKED BLACK PEPPER ➤ PARMESAN CRISPS

I'm always the one picking the crispy burnt cheese off the sides of onion soup crocks. So what could be better than a whole bowl of crispy cheese? It's the perfect snack.

> 2 CUPS (200 G) SHREDDED PARMESAN
>
> 1 TABLESPOON FRESHLY CRACKED BLACK PEPPER

1. Preheat the oven to 350°F (180°C).

2. Line a 12 x 18-inch (30 x 45-cm) baking sheet with foil and coat lightly with nonstick spray.

3. Spread the Parmesan onto the baking sheet. Make sure that it's spread evenly, or your crisps won't bake evenly. Sprinkle with the black pepper and bake for 15 to 20 minutes, or until the cheese has turned a uniform deep golden brown.

4. Remove from the oven and let cool. Once it's cool enough to handle, remove the cheese from the foil and crack it into rough, bite-sized pieces. Store in an airtight container in a cool, dry place.

> *YIELD: 1 (12 X 18-INCH [30 X 45-CM]) PAN*

CURRIED CHIVE POPCORN

Popcorn in any form is addictive. I've long been a fan of any kind of popcorn where the seasoning mix cakes onto your fingers and then you have to lick it all off, one finger at a time. Disgusting? Perhaps...but I know I'm not the only one. This is that kind of popcorn.

> 2 BAGS PLAIN MICROWAVE POPCORN, POPPED ACCORDING TO PACKAGE DIRECTIONS
>
> ¼ CUP (59 ML) OLIVE OIL
>
> 4 TEASPOONS CURRY POWDER
>
> 4 TEASPOONS CHILI POWDER
>
> 2 TEASPOONS FINE SEA SALT
>
> 2 TABLESPOONS FREEZE-DRIED CHIVES

While it's still hot, pour the popcorn into a large, clean paper bag. Drizzle with the oil and add the spices. Fold the top of the bag a couple of times and shake the bag vigorously to coat. Pour into serving bowls. Store leftovers in an airtight container in a cool, dry place.

> *YIELD: 8 CUPS (174 G)*

KIX MIX ▾

I expanded on this recipe from the 1950s that used Kix as a savory snack.

1 TABLESPOON GARLIC POWDER

½ TABLESPOON ONION POWDER

1 TABLESPOON SALT

½ TABLESPOON FRESHLY GROUND BLACK PEPPER

1 TABLESPOON DRIED BASIL

1½ CUPS (32 G) KIX CEREAL

1½ CUPS (32 G) CRACKLIN' OAT BRAN CEREAL

1 CUP (22 G) LIFE CEREAL

6 TABLESPOONS (86 G) UNSALTED BUTTER

1. Preheat the oven to 350°F (180°C).

2. In a small bowl, combine the garlic and onion powders, salt, pepper, and basil.

3. Pour the cereals into a large bowl. Melt the butter and drizzle it over the cereals. Quickly add the spice mix and toss well to coat. Spread the cereal mixture evenly onto a 12 x 18-inch (30 x 45-cm) baking sheet and place it in the middle of the oven. Bake for 20 to 30 minutes, stirring twice so the edges don't burn.

4. Remove from the oven and let cool before serving. Store in an airtight container in a cool, dry place.

YIELD: 4 CUPS (88 G)

MIDDLE EASTERN SPICED ALMONDS

Nuts are quintessential bar snacks, and this book wouldn't be complete without a nut recipe. Almonds are one of my favorites, and dried fruit adds a nice balance to the recipe.

4 CUPS (572 G) RAW WHOLE ALMONDS

2 TABLESPOONS BUTTER, MELTED

4 TEASPOONS KOSHER SALT

4 TEASPOONS LIGHT BROWN SUGAR

4 TEASPOONS GARAM MASALA*

1 TABLESPOON CURRY POWDER

1½ CUPS (243 G) GOLDEN RAISINS

1. Preheat the oven to 350°F (180°C).

2. Spread the almonds evenly on a 12 x 18-inch (30 x 45-cm) baking sheet and place it in the center of the oven for 15 minutes.

3. Mix the butter, salt, sugar, and spices together in a large bowl and slide the hot nuts in as soon as they come out of the oven. Add the raisins and toss well to coat. Let cool before serving.

YIELD: 4 CUPS (572 G)

*See the description of garam masala on page 101.

WASABI PEA CARAMEL CORN ➤

Caramel corn is a snack that evokes childhood for me, as I'm sure it does for a lot of people. The wasabi peas in this recipe pull it in a more grown-up direction. The sweet, savory, and spicy preparation pairs well with orange notes. Try it with the Calvados Cocktail on page 62.

2 BAGS PLAIN MICROWAVE POPCORN, POPPED ACCORDING
    TO PACKAGE DIRECTIONS

1 CUP (225 G) DARK BROWN SUGAR

½ CUP (119 mL) LIGHT CORN SYRUP

½ CUP (114 G) BUTTER

2 TEASPOONS KOSHER SALT, DIVIDED

½ TEASPOON BAKING SODA

1 TEASPOON VANILLA EXTRACT

2 CUPS (320 G) WASABI PEAS

1. Preheat the oven to 250°F (120°C). Line a 12 x 18-inch (30 x 45-cm) baking sheet with foil and spray it with nonstick spray.

2. Place the popcorn in a large bowl.

3. Combine the brown sugar, corn syrup, butter, and 1 teaspoon of the salt in a large saucepan and place it over high heat. Cook, stirring, until the butter has melted and the mixture becomes smooth. Lower the heat to medium and let boil for 5 minutes. Remove from the heat and stir in the baking soda and vanilla. (The mixture will foam a bit and become cloudy when the baking soda is stirred in.) Quickly pour the caramel over the popcorn, add 1 cup (160 g) of the wasabi peas, and stir well and quickly to coat.

4. Spread the popcorn evenly onto the prepared baking sheet and place it in the center of the oven. Bake for 45 minutes. Remove the pan from the oven, sprinkle with the remaining 1 cup (160 g) of peas and 1 teaspoon of salt, and let cool. When it's cool, remove the popcorn from the foil and break it into bite-sized pieces. Store in an airtight container in a cool, dry place.

YIELD: 8 CUPS (174 G)

Pickled Snacks

AMERICANS, AS A WHOLE, ARE FAMILIAR WITH PICKLING ONLY ONE FOOD
—the cucumber. That's an interesting fact, since pickled foods have been in existence
for about four thousand years. Of course, for the many millennia before refrigeration,
pickling was a necessity in that the acidic nature of the various brines helped to
preserve foods (see Shrubs, page 149).

With the advent of electricity and, eventually, refrigeration, pickling became more of
a hobby—something your aunt with the really big garden did every fall. And while it
never faded into obscurity, it certainly lost its place at the head of the table.

Nowadays, as the food movement steers itself back toward small organic farms and
sustainability, we find that many of the old practices are once again in vogue.

Pickling is relevant again in the United States. Many fine restaurants now pickle not
only vegetables but also meats and fish. The beauty of pickling as it pertains to bar
snacks, aside from the deliciousness, is the ease of preparing these snacks in bulk
weeks in advance. You'll never have to go without a snack pairing for your cocktail
again…hurrah!

PICKLED KIELBASA

*Before refrigeration, pickling was used to preserve meat. Nowadays we pickle meats
for the flavor alone…it's a wonderful combination, the fats of the meat mingling with
the sharpness of the vinegar brine. I chose a smoky meat to pair with a fairly simple,
sweeter brine.*

> 1½ POUNDS (681 G) SMOKED KIELBASA,
>   SLICED INTO 1-INCH (2.5-CM) PIECES
>
> 1 SMALL ONION, THINLY SLICED
>
> 1 CUP (237 ML) DISTILLED WHITE VINEGAR
>
> 1 CUP (237 ML) WATER
>
> ¾ CUP (169 G) DARK BROWN SUGAR
>
> 1 TABLESPOON KOSHER SALT

1. In a clean 1-quart (948 mL) mason jar, layer the kielbasa and onion.

2. Pour the vinegar and water into a saucepan and add the brown sugar and salt. Place
over high heat and bring to a boil, stirring to dissolve the sugar. Reduce the heat and let

simmer for 5 minutes. Remove from the heat and let cool completely. Pour the cool liquid into the mason jar and seal. Refrigerate for at least one day and up to one month.

YIELD: 1½ POUNDS (681 G) SLICED KIELBASA

PICKLED RADISHES WITH SONOMA SALT

We were in Sonoma at our friend James McNair's house one weekend (James is the king of the one-subject cookbook), and he put out some radishes from his garden, a small bowl of water, and another small bowl of salt. It's one of those small food memories that stands out in my mind. Here's my version of James's radishes.

2 CUPS (474 ML) SEASONED RICE WINE VINEGAR

1 CUP (200 G) SUGAR

1 TABLESPOON KOSHER SALT

1 TABLESPOON BLACK PEPPERCORNS

2 TEASPOONS CUMIN SEEDS

1 TEASPOON WHOLE CLOVES

2 BAY LEAVES

2 DOZEN SPRING RADISHES*, SUCH AS FRENCH BREAKFAST

SONOMA SALT (RECIPE FOLLOWS)

1. Pour the vinegar into a saucepan and add the sugar, salt, peppercorns, cumin seeds, cloves, and bay leaves. Bring to a boil, stir to dissolve the sugar, and remove from the heat.

2. Clean the radishes, leaving a bit of the stem if possible. Place them in a clean 1-quart (948 mL) mason jar and pour the brine over them. Seal the jar and refrigerate for at least 24 hours and up to one month.

*Spring radishes tend to be smaller, ideal for pickling.

YIELD: 24 RADISHES

SONOMA SALT

¼ CUP (75 G) GOOD-QUALITY FINE SEA SALT*

1 TEASPOON SUGAR

1 TEASPOON DRIED TARRAGON, CRUSHED FINE

Mix the ingredients together well. Serve in a small bowl on the side of the pickled radishes.

*Sea salt comes from a wide variety of regions and in a lot of colors. For extra punch, try a red Hawaiian sea salt.

ROSEMARY GARLIC PICKLED EGGS ➤

The hardest part about pickling eggs isn't the pickling—it's the hard boiling. Many people tend to boil their eggs too long, resulting in that greenish color surrounding the yolk. While it doesn't greatly affect the taste of the yolk, it's not particularly attractive. Follow the directions below, and you'll wind up with perfectly hard-boiled eggs.

6 LARGE EGGS

1 CUP (237 mL) DISTILLED WHITE VINEGAR

1 CUP (237 mL) WATER

½ CUP (100 G) SUGAR

1 HEAD GARLIC, CLOVES SEPARATED AND PEELED

5 FRESH ROSEMARY SPRIGS

1 TABLESPOON PICKLING SPICE

1 TEASPOON KOSHER SALT

1. Arrange the eggs in a single layer in a saucepan and cover them by at least 1 inch with cold water. Place the pan over medium heat and cook until the water comes to a boil. Boil for 1 minute, remove from the heat, and cover for 12 minutes. At this point, you should have perfect hard-boiled eggs. Drain the water and fill the pan with ice water to cool down the eggs. When they are cool enough to handle, peel the eggs and place them in a clean 1-quart (948 mL) mason jar.

2. Combine the vinegar, water, sugar, garlic, rosemary, pickling spice, and salt in another saucepan and place it over high heat. Bring to a boil, stir to dissolve the sugar, and remove from the heat. When cool enough to handle, pull out the rosemary sprigs and insert them into the mason jar, being careful not to poke the eggs. Pour the remaining liquid into the jar to cover the eggs. Seal the jar and refrigerate for at least one day and up to one month.

YIELD: 6 EGGS

SHRIMP ESCABECHE

Escabeche is most commonly known as a Mediterranean dish usually consisting of poached fish in an acidic solution. It's a little less pungent than most pickled dishes due to the smaller amount of acid and the addition of oil. It makes an excellent bar snack served with something crisp as an accompaniment.

½ CUP (119 mL) WHITE WINE VINEGAR

2 TABLESPOONS SUGAR

1 TEASPOON KOSHER SALT

1 TABLESPOON FENNEL SEEDS

½ TEASPOON CRUSHED RED PEPPER FLAKES

½ CINNAMON STICK

1 CUP (237 mL) EXTRA VIRGIN OLIVE OIL

3 CLOVES GARLIC

1 RED BELL PEPPER, SEEDED AND SLICED INTO ¼-INCH (6-MM) STRIPS

1 SMALL RED ONION, PEELED, HALVED, AND THINLY SLICED

1 POUND (454 G) LARGE SHRIMP (ABOUT 20–25), PEELED AND DEVEINED

1. Combine the vinegar, sugar, salt, fennel seeds, crushed red pepper, and cinnamon stick in a saucepan and bring to a simmer. Remove from the heat and pour into a nonreactive bowl. Let cool.

2. Pour the olive oil into a small saucepan and add the garlic. Bring to a simmer and immediately remove from the heat so as not to brown the garlic.

3. Add the bell pepper, onion, and garlic oil to the vinegar mixture and set aside.

4. Bring a large pot of lightly salted water to a boil and quickly drop in the shrimp. Cook for no longer than 5 minutes. Drain and place in an ice bath to stop the cooking process.

5. Add the shrimp to the bowl with vinegar mixture and toss well. Cover and refrigerate overnight before serving.

YIELD: APPROXIMATELY 25 SHRIMP

Small Plate Snacks

SMALL PLATE DINING CAUGHT ON HERE IN THE STATES BACK AROUND 2000, and many people thought something new and exciting had been discovered. Truth be told, southern Europeans have been eating like that for many years. In Spain, it's called tapas, and in Turkey and Greece, it's called mezzes. Small plates are sexy and exciting, and it's a way to try an array of foods in one sitting.

Due once again to my philosophy about simplicity when it comes to bar snacks, these recipes are as far as I'll go toward small plates and what I think of as "bar food." Some of the recipes may be a stretch in terms of true small-plate fare but I've included them in this section because they're a little more substantial and a little more labor intensive.

Choosing at least one of these items and pairing it with a few of the snacks from the other sections will give you a well-balanced cocktail party.

BAKED GOAT CHEESE

If you like goat cheese, make this one of your go-to recipes. You can take this from refrigerator to table in 20 minutes and impress the hell out of your friends in the bargain.

> 2 CUPS (300 G) CRUMBLED GOAT CHEESE
>
> 2 TABLESPOONS OLIVE OIL
>
> 1 SMALL ONION, THINLY SLICED
>
> ½ CUP (74 G) DRIED MISSION FIGS (ABOUT 6)
>
> ½ TEASPOON DRIED THYME
>
> ½ TEASPOON KOSHER SALT
>
> 3 GRINDS FRESH BLACK PEPPER
>
> ¼ CUP (59 ML) DRY WHITE WINE

1. Preheat the oven to 375°F (190°C).

2. Place the goat cheese in a small, oven-safe casserole dish.

3. Pour the oil into a small skillet and place it over medium heat. Add the sliced onion and sauté until the onion is limp and beginning to brown, about 5 to 7 minutes.

4. Thinly slice the figs and add them to the skillet along with the thyme, salt, and pepper. Stir and add the wine. Simmer until the pan is mostly dry.

(continued on next page)

5. Spread the fig mixture over the goat cheese and place the casserole dish in the oven for 15 minutes or until the cheese begins to bubble.

6. Remove from the oven and serve immediately with a crusty sliced baguette.

YIELD: APPROXIMATELY 3 CUPS (450 G)

BEER CHEESE PUFFS

The dough in this recipe is the same as that used to make cream puffs and éclairs—it's called a pâte à choux. It's essentially cooked twice—once on the stovetop, and then again in the oven, where the water turns to steam and leaves the air pockets that make the snack so light. They're really best eaten right out of the oven, and you don't have to worry about what to do with the leftovers…there won't be any.

1 CUP (237 mL) BEER (ALE OR LAGER)

1 TEASPOON SALT

4 OUNCES (114 G) UNSALTED BUTTER, CHILLED AND CUT INTO BITS

1 CUP (121 G) ALL-PURPOSE FLOUR

4 LARGE EGGS

½ CUP (50 G) GRATED SHARP CHEDDAR CHEESE

¼ CUP (25 G) GRATED ROMANO CHEESE

2 GRINDS FRESH BLACK PEPPER

COARSE KOSHER SALT, FOR TOPPING

1. Preheat the oven to 425°F (220°C).

2. Pour the beer, salt, and butter into a saucepan and bring to a simmer. Once the butter has melted, remove the pan from the heat and add the flour all at once. Stir well to blend and return the pan to the heat. Stir well to dry the dough out a bit—it will pull away from the sides of the pan and form a ball. Remove from the heat and, using an electric mixer, quickly blend in the eggs, one at a time.* Fold in the cheeses and black pepper.

3. Spray 2 (12 x 18-inch [30 x 45-cm]) baking sheets with nonstick spray and drop the dough onto the sheets by the tablespoonful, leaving about 2 inches (5 cm) between each ball. Top with the kosher salt and place in the oven. Bake for 20 to 25 minutes, until the dough has puffed and turned golden brown. Remove from the oven and serve immediately. These are best eaten right away.

You have to be really quick with this step, as you don't want to cook the eggs as you add them to the hot dough.

YIELD: APPROXIMATELY 40 CHEESE PUFFS

CHEESY MONKEY BREAD

Monkey bread is traditionally a sticky, sweet, pull-apart bread…and I'll forgo the usual joke about there being no monkeys in the recipe. The origin of the name is actually uncertain—some say that the silent film star and comedienne ZaSu Pitts named it.

My version is filled with cheese, herbs, and spices. It is, of course, still a pull-apart bread, and it's perfect to set down in a group of friends. Serve it right out of the oven for best results, and use any leftovers the next morning at breakfast—it's great with eggs.

1 CUP (237 mL) PLUS 3 TABLESPOONS (45 mL) WATER, BOILING

2¼ TEASPOONS DRY YEAST

2½ TEASPOONS KOSHER SALT

1½ TEASPOONS SUGAR

3¼ CUPS (393 G) ALL-PURPOSE FLOUR

3 TABLESPOONS SHREDDED MOZZARELLA CHEESE

2 TABLESPOONS SHREDDED PARMESAN CHEESE

1 TEASPOON FRESHLY GROUND BLACK PEPPER

1 TEASPOON DRIED BASIL

¼ TEASPOON DRIED THYME

2 TABLESPOONS EXTRA VIRGIN OLIVE OIL

8 TABLESPOONS (114 G) BUTTER

MONKEY BREAD COATING (RECIPE FOLLOWS)

1. Pour the boiling water into a large bowl and let it cool to lukewarm (110°F [43°C]) before adding the yeast, salt, and sugar. Give the yeast 5 minutes to bloom.

2. In a separate bowl, combine the flour, mozzarella, parmesan, pepper, basil, and thyme.

3. Add the flour mixture to the yeast mixture all at once. Add the olive oil and stir with a wooden spoon until a dough begins to form. You may have to wet your hands and finish mixing by hand to incorporate all of the flour.

4. Loosely cover the dough and set it in a warm place to rise. Once it has doubled in volume, it is ready to form.*

5. Preheat the oven to 350°F (180°C).

6. Prepare a loaf pan by spraying with nonstick spray.

7. Pinch off roughly 50 pieces of dough, each about the size of a ping-pong ball, and roll each ball until smooth. Melt the butter. Dip each ball into the butter and then roll it in the monkey bread coating. Place the balls into the loaf pan, making sure not to press down on them.   *(continued on next page)*

8. Let the dough rise for 20 minutes. Place the loaf pan in the center of the oven and bake for 45 minutes. Remove from the oven and let cool for 10 minutes before popping out of the pan. Serve warm, on a large plate. Guests can use their fingers to pull the monkey bread apart.

YIELD: 1 LOAF

You may refrigerate the dough at this point for up to 2 days or use it immediately.

MONKEY BREAD COATING

1½ CUPS (150 G) GRATED ROMANO CHEESE

¾ TEASPOON SMOKED PAPRIKA

¾ TEASPOON DRIED THYME

1½ TEASPOONS KOSHER SALT

¾ TEASPOON BLACK PEPPER

Combine all the ingredients in a medium bowl and set aside.

LAMB KEFTA

I've long been a fan of Middle Eastern food. When I lived in NYC years ago, this food had the dual advantage of being really tasty and really cheap—which fit my meager budget perfectly. I'd often get falafel or kefta and eat them as I walked to work. They're perfect street food—which also makes them perfect bar snacks. Kefta is, in its simplest form, ground meat and spices. I use lamb—if you don't like lamb, try substituting ground beef. I also suggest two different cooking techniques, but I strongly recommend the grill.

1 POUND (454 G) GROUND LAMB

1½ TABLESPOONS GRATED ONION

1 TABLESPOON ALL-PURPOSE FLOUR

2 TEASPOONS GARAM MASALA

1½ TEASPOONS KOSHER SALT

½ TEASPOON GROUND CINNAMON

½ TEASPOON DRIED OREGANO

YOGURT DIPPING SAUCE (RECIPE FOLLOWS)

1. Fire up your grill or, alternatively, preheat the oven to 400°F (200°C).

2. Put the lamb into a large bowl and add all of the remaining ingredients. Add 3 tablespoons (45 mL) of water and mix well by hand.

3. Drop the mixture by the tablespoonful onto a 12 x 18-inch (30 x 45-cm) baking sheet and roll each piece into a log shape about 3 inches (7.5 cm) long.

4. If grilling, place the lamb over the hottest part of the grill and cook for a total of 5 minutes, making sure to turn and grill on all sides. Keep in mind that ground lamb is fatty and will most likely cause flames. Stay armed with long tongs and move the kefta out of the flames as needed to prevent burning.

5. If using the oven, place the kefta on a baking sheet and bake for 8 minutes.

6. Serve the kefta warm, with Yogurt Dipping Sauce on the side. Kefta are best served right from the grill. They do not reheat well.

YIELD: 16 PIECES

YOGURT DIPPING SAUCE

½ CUP (119 mL) GREEK YOGURT

1 TEASPOON FINELY CHOPPED FRESH MINT

½ TEASPOON GARAM MASALA

½ TEASPOON FRESH LEMON JUICE

PINCH KOSHER SALT

Mix all the ingredients together in a small bowl. Refrigerate until ready to serve.

LEMON MAPLE COCKTAIL RIBS

I like baby back ribs for this recipe, as they tend to be meatier. You'll have to ask your butcher to cut the ribs lengthwise for you. Of course, you could always try cutting through them with a hacksaw, like I did the first time I made them…but I wouldn't suggest it!

BARBECUE SAUCE*

1 CUP (237 mL) PURE MAPLE SYRUP

1 CUP (237 mL) TOMATO PASTE

ZEST OF 1 LEMON

JUICE OF 1 LEMON

¼ CUP (59 mL) WHITE VINEGAR

½ TEASPOON CAYENNE PEPPER

1 TABLESPOON KOSHER SALT

1 TEASPOON BLACK PEPPER

RIBS

1 RACK BABY BACK RIBS, CUT IN HALF LENGTHWISE

SALT AND PEPPER TO TASTE

LEMON ZEST (FOR GARNISH)

(continued on next page)

1. Preheat the oven to 275°F (140°C).

2. In a bowl, whisk together all the Barbecue Sauce ingredients.

3. Season the ribs with salt and pepper and sear both sides in a hot pan. Place the ribs in a baking dish and cover with Barbecue Sauce. Bake for 2½ hours, or until really tender. Remove the ribs from the oven and let stand until cool enough to handle. Using a very sharp knife, cut the ribs into individual portions and serve garnished with a little lemon zest.

*You'll find that this sauce is intentionally thinner than most barbecue sauces.

> *YIELD: APPROXIMATELY 20 RIBS*

POUTINE ▾

Poutine is Acadian slang for mushy mess…and it couldn't be more delicious. The authentic version presents a bit of a problem for the typical American home cook, in that cheese curds are hard to purchase. I live in the Midwest, home of the cheese curd, and even I can't find it in most markets. To that end, I've substituted part-skim, low-moisture mozzarella—it's not perfect but it's not a bad substitute—but if you can get your hands on some cheese curds by all means use them.

2 LARGE IDAHO POTATOES

SUNFLOWER OIL FOR FRYING

SALT TO TASTE

4 OUNCES (114 G) PART-SKIM, LOW-MOISTURE MOZZARELLA, CUT
    INTO ½-INCH (14-MM) CUBES

½ CUP (119 ML) BLACK PEPPER GRAVY (RECIPE FOLLOWS)

4 OUNCES (114 G) SHREDDED CHICKEN (OPTIONAL)

1. Scrub the potatoes well and cut them into ½-inch (14 mm) fry shapes. Soak them in ice water for at least 30 minutes.

2. Preheat the sunflower oil to 325°F (160°C).* Drain the potatoes and pat them dry so as not to spatter yourself with hot oil. Drop the potatoes into the oil, making sure not to crowd them. Fry for about 10 minutes or until the potatoes are a little limp. Transfer them from the oil to a paper towel–lined plate. Let them rest for 10 to 20 minutes.

3. Preheat the oven to 350°F (180°C).

4. Raise the oil temperature to 350°F (180°C) and fry the potatoes a second time until crisp and golden brown, about 3 minutes. Remove the fries from the oil and season them right away with salt.

5. Pile the fries in an oven-safe dish and scatter the cheese cubes over the top. Bake for 2 to 3 minutes, until the cheese begins to get soft; do not to let it melt completely.

6. Remove the dish from the oven and top with the Black Pepper Gravy and shredded chicken, if desired. Serve immediately.

See Deep-Fried Snacks, page 153.

BLACK PEPPER GRAVY

4 TABLESPOONS (57 G) UNSALTED BUTTER

3 TABLESPOONS (23 G) ALL-PURPOSE FLOUR

1½ CUPS (356 ML) MILK, SCALDED

¾ TEASPOON KOSHER SALT

5 GRINDS FRESH BLACK PEPPER

SPLASH BEER

Melt the butter in a medium saucepan, and whisk in the flour all at once. Cook for 1 minute. Whisk in the milk a little at a time, adding more as the gravy thickens. Season with the salt and pepper and a splash of beer. Simmer for 1 minute and remove from the heat. Use immediately or cover the top of the gravy directly with plastic wrap to prevent a skin from forming.

SAVORY POP-TART

Who doesn't love a Pop-Tart? These are mini versions, and while, yes, I did go for the kitsch factor with these, they're still excellent bar snacks. The added advantage is that they can be made in advance and frozen. Reheat them in the oven or…you guessed it: the toaster!

CRUST

2½ cups (303 g) all-purpose flour

1 teaspoon salt

7 tablespoons (100 g) unsalted butter, chilled and cut into bits

7 tablespoons (100 g) vegetable shortening, chilled and cut into bits

6 tablespoons (90 mL) ice water

FILLING

2 tablespoons olive oil

1 small onion, thinly sliced

1 pound (454 g) Mexican chorizo

Pinch dried oregano

Pinch ground cinnamon

¼ cup (29 g) shredded queso blanco

For the Crust

1. In a food processor, combine the flour, salt, butter, and shortening and process until the butter and shortening have broken down into small bits. Transfer the mixture to a large bowl and slowly add the ice water, stirring with a fork. Form the dough into a ball and chill for 1 hour before rolling out.

2. Split the dough into two portions and roll out each of them on a well-floured board to a ¹/₈-inch (3-mm) thickness. Cut the dough into 2 x 4–inch (5 x 10-cm) rectangles. Place the rectangles on a 12 x 18-inch (30 x 45-cm) baking sheet with parchment between the layers. Freeze for at least 20 minutes.

For the Filling

1. Pour the olive oil into a large skillet and set it over medium heat. Add the onions and sauté until limp, about 5 to 7 minutes. Add the chorizo, oregano, and cinnamon and sauté, breaking up the meat with a spoon, for another 7 minutes. Remove from the heat and pour into a strainer set over a bowl. Press down on the chorizo mixture to remove as much grease as possible. Let the meat rest in the strainer until cool, then transfer it to a bowl and mix in the cheese.

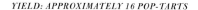

To Assemble

1. Preheat the oven to 350°F (180°C).

2. Place 6 of the rectangles on a flat surface and place 1 heaping teaspoon of the chorizo mixture on each one, spreading to within ¼ inch (6 mm) of the edges. Brush 6 more rectangles with egg wash on one side and place one rectangle on top of each of the 6 filled pieces. Press down on the edges to seal, and crimp with a fork. Repeat with the remaining pieces.

3. Place all the Pop-Tarts on baking sheets, brush them with egg wash, pierce the tops decoratively with a fork, and bake until golden brown. Serve immediately or let them cool and store, refrigerated, in an airtight container.

4. Reheat for 10 minutes in a 350°F (180°C) oven before serving. These also freeze very well.

YIELD: APPROXIMATELY 16 POP-TARTS

TOASTS

THE ACT OF RAISING A CUP IS ANCIENT. IT IS BELIEVED THAT PARTY
animal Attila the Hun would offer no fewer than three toasts per course. The Saxons
shouted *"Waes hael!"* which meant "be of health" and later became "wassail," and
I can't tell you how much easier Christmas caroling will be for me now that I know
what the hell I'm singing about. As far as the Vikings are concerned, there seems
to be a lot of controversy as to whether the toast *"Skaal!"* was made while quaffing
from the actual *skulls* of enemies.

The term "toast" seems to find its roots in the 1600s. A chunk of spiced toast
would be left to steep in a goblet of acidic wine in order to improve the wine's flavor.
Even Falstaff requests that the barkeep "put a toast in't" in Shakespeare's *The Merry
Wives of Windsor*.

And then there's this quote from a 1709 issue of *The Tatler:* "A celebrated beauty
of those times was in the Cross Bath, and one of the crowd of her admirers took a
glass of the water and drank her health. A gay fellow, half fuddled, offered to jump
in, and swore though he liked not the liquor, he would have the toast." And that
celebrated beauty became the "toast of the town." Get it?

With such a rich history, it seems a shame that toasts are now relegated to fits of
awkward discomfort at your cousin's wedding. So gather round my public bath and
raise your goblets, my half-fuddled friends, because it's time to take back the toast.

As an event planner, I stress that toasts act as the party's mile markers. There is a
time at most events that requires your guests' focus, whether it is to thank the host

for the meal or to put the spotlight on the bride and groom for the cake cutting. But don't feel as if you need a big room or an important event to raise your voice; a brief and witty toast can be hugely impactful when sincere. Five words: "Here's lookin' at you, kid."

Who among us can say with sincerity that we don't long to have a touch of Dorothy Parker? The image of that sharp-witted, sharp-tongued group sparring at the Algonquin Round Table over…well…Algonquins (see page 42) carries a jaded sophistication that pairs as well with cocktails as salted peanuts. To help you channel your inner Algonquin, I've assembled some how-to tips here to prep you before you interrupt the room and raise your glass:

- ✦ Be in keeping with the occasion.

- ✦ Sit, stand: whatever makes you comfortable.

- ✦ Make eye contact with everyone at the table.

- ✦ Keep your toast short and to the point.

- ✦ No rapping on wine glasses with silverware for attention. This is not Attica.

- ✦ Toasts are usually at the beginning of a meal, but spontaneous toasts are always fun when appropriate. Just don't make a long-winded speech as the host is about to bring hot food to the table.

- ✦ When toasted, don't drink to yourself; graciously acknowledge the toast with a "thank you."

- ✦ When someone else is toasting, do not drain your glass; there may be another toast immediately following.

- ✦ Likewise, no matter how early you're handed a glass, no furtive sipping before the toast.

- ✦ Toasting with a non-alcoholic beverage is perfectly acceptable. Water is OK unless you're at a Navy event, in which case the superstition is that you're sending the honoree to a watery grave, so…

- ✦ Finish your toast on a positive note. No one wants to drink to a bummer.

- ✦ Clearly define the end with a raised glass and a "Cheers!"
- ✦ Lastly, none of my cocktails here, not one, calls for slamming an inverted glass down on the bar top.

My favorite toast was taught to me in Tuscany. We were in a villa at an oversized table littered with fava bean pods and Pecorino when the host raised a glass and said *"Toccato Uno, Taccato Tutti."* This translates to "Touch one, touch all." You know how you strain across the table to reach everyone and then you keep missing one person and you get nervous about them feeling slighted? This lets you off the hook. The sentiment is that by touching one glass, I've basically got the rest of you, too. The perfect toast; leave it to the Italians to be gracious but not waste any valuable time when there's food on the table.

The vast majority of the toasts I have gathered are old standards; the most beautiful and simply introspective ones are frequently Irish. I have assembled some of history's greatest one-liners (organized by category to help you find the perfect sentiment) and urge you to commit your favorite to memory…or at the very least, to the palm of your hand. I expect you to impress me next time we're at the bar.

Love

"Here's to love, the only fire against which there is no insurance."

"Here's to love, that begins with a fever and ends with a yawn."

"Here's to moderation in all things—except in love."

"Let's drink to love—which is nothing, unless it's divided by two."

"May we have those in our arms who we love in our hearts."

"May we kiss those we please, and please those we kiss."

"Drink to me only with thine eyes, and I will pledge with mine; or leave a kiss but in the cup, and I'll not look for wine."

"Here's to the land we love and the love we land."

*"A drink, my lass, in a deep clear glass, just properly tempered by ice,
and here's to the lips mine have kissed, and if they were thine, here's twice."*

"Here's to love—it doesn't make the world go 'round, but it makes the ride
worthwhile."

Women

*"Drink to the fair woman, whom I think is most entitled to it,
for if anything ever can drive me to drink, she certainly can do it."*

"To woman—the fairest work of the great author; the edition is large and
no man should be without a copy."

*"Here's to woman! Would that we could fall into her arms without falling
into her hands."*

"Here's to all of the women who have used me and abused me; and may
they continue to do so!"

Drinking

"May wine never prove the cause of strife."

"Here's to the rapturous, wild, and ineffable pleasure of drinking at
somebody else's expense."

*"Here's to champagne, the drink divine, that makes us forget our troubles;
it's made of a dollar's worth of wine and three dollars' worth of bubbles."*

"The bubble winked at me and said 'You'll miss me, brother, when
you're dead.'"

*"Don't die of love in heaven above or hell, they'll not endure you.
Why look so glum when Doctor Rum is waiting for to cure you?"*

"Beer is proof that God loves us and wants us to be happy."

"Give me a woman who loves beer and I will conquer the world."

"A bottle at night and business in the morning."

"Here's to the temperance supper, with water in glasses tall,
  And coffee and tea to end with—and me not there at all."

Cheeky

"Here's to the pictures on my desk. May they never meet."

"Here's to the bachelor who's decided to take a wife—but hasn't yet
  decided whose."

"Here's to being single, drinking doubles, and seeing triple."

"Here's to you as good as you are and here's to me as bad as I am. As good
  as you are and as bad as I am—I'm as good as you are as bad as I am."

"May you die at age ninety, shot by the jealous husband of a teenager."

"Here's to a long life and a merry one, a quick death and an easy one,
  a good girl and a pretty one, a cold beer and another one."

"There's a health to poverty; it sticks by us when all friends forsake us."

"I like to have a martini, two at the very most. After three I'm under
  the table, after four I'm under my host!"

"Early to rise and early to bed makes a man healthy and wealthy
  and dead."

"To work, the curse of the drinking class!"

"Here's to keeping your eye on the doughnut, not on the hole."

"Here's to the men of all classes,
  Who through lasses and glasses,
  Will make themselves asses."

Life

"Here's to today! For tomorrow we may be radioactive." (1950s toast)

"May you live as long as you want to and may you want to as long as you live."

"Here's hoping that you live forever and mine is the last voice you hear."

"May your coffin be of 100-year-old oak, and may we plant the tree together, tomorrow."

"May you live all the days of your life."

"To the old, long life and treasure; to the young, all health and pleasure."

"May every hair on your head turn into a candle to light your way to heaven, and may God and His Holy Mother take the harm of the years away from you."

"Here's to growing old; many are denied the privilege."

"May the Lord love us but not call us too soon."

"So live that when you come to die, even the undertaker will feel sorry for you."

Death

"Though life is now pleasant and sweet to the sense, we'll be damnably mouldy a hundred years hence."

"May we all come to peaceful ends, and leave our debts unto our friends."

"Here's to other meetings and merry greetings then; and here's to those we've drunk with but never can again."

"Stand to your glasses steady! 'Tis all we have left to prize. A cup to the dead already; 'Hurrah' for the next that dies."

"May our lives, like the leaves of the maple, grow more beautiful as they fade. May we say our farewells, when it's time to go, all smiling and unafraid."

"Here's to the undertakers—may they never overtake us!"

Friendship

"Here's champagne to my real friends; and a real pain to my sham friends."

"To get the full value of joy, you must have someone to divide it with."

"May the hinges of friendship never rust, or the wings of love lose a feather."

"Who is a friend but someone to toast, someone to gibe, someone to roast. My friends are the best friends, loyal, willing and able. Now let's get to drinking! Glasses off the table!"

"A glass is good, and a lass is good,
And a pipe to smoke in cold weather;
The world is good and the people are good,
And we're all good fellows together."

"I've drank to your health in taverns, I've drank to your health in my home, I've drank to your health so damn many times, I believe I've ruined my own!"

"There are good ships, there are wood ships, there are ships that sail the sea. But the best ships, are friendships, and may they always be."

"Here's to eternity—may we spend it in as good company as this night finds us."

"Here's to our friends—in the hopes that they, wherever they are, are drinking to us."

"To our absent friends: although they are out of sight, we recognize them with our glasses."

Curses

"May a band of gypsies camp in your belly and train bears to dance on your liver."

"May the devil make a ladder of your backbone while he is picking apples in the garden of hell."

"Here's to those who love us well—those who don't may go to hell."

Blessings

"May good fortune follow you all your life and never catch up with you."

"May every mirror we look at cast an honest reflection."

"May we be happy and our enemies know it."

"May your right hand always be stretched out in friendship, never in want."

"May you get all your wishes but one, so you always have something to strive for."

"May the best day you have seen be worse than your worst to come."

"May your glass be ever full. May the roof over your head be always strong. And may you be in heaven half an hour before the devil knows you're dead."

"May the roof above us never fall in and may the friends gathered below it never fall out."

"Here's luck! For we know not where we are going."

"May your pockets be heavy and your heart be light. May good luck pursue you each morning and night."

"When climbing the hill of prosperity, may we never meet a friend coming down."

"Now, down with care and blithely swear a truce to melancholy; Let each good soul fill up his bowl and drink a toast to folly."

Hosts

"To our hostess. She's a gem. We love her, God bless her. And the devil take her husband."

"To our host, who has the ability to make us all feel at home, even though that's where he wishes we were."

"Here's to our guest, don't let him rest, but keep his elbow bending. 'Tis time to drink, full time to think tomorrow…when you're mending."

"To our host, a most excellent man; for is not a man fairly judged by the company he keeps?"

"To our friend, who is neither an optimist who sees a glass as half full, nor a pessimist who sees a glass as half empty; but a host, who sees it as a glass that needs topping off."

Long and Beautiful

"Were't the last drop in the well, as I gasped upon the brink; 'ere my fainting spirit fell, 'tis to thee that I would drink."

"We may live without poetry, music and art;
We may live without conscience, and live without heart;
We may live without friends; we may live without books;
But civilized man cannot live without cooks.
We may live without books—what is knowledge but grieving?
We may live without hope—what is hope but deceiving?
We may live without love—what is passion but pining?
But where is the man that can live without dining?"

*"Come in the evening or come in the morning;
Come when you're looked for or come without warning;
A thousand welcomes you'll find here before you.
The oftener you come here the more I'll adore you."*

"I fill this cup to one made up
   Of loveliness alone,
A woman, of her gentle sex,
   The seeming paragon;
To whom the better elements
   And kindly stars have given
A form so fair that, like the air,
   'Tis less of earth than heaven."

"Here's a health to the future; a sigh for the past.
We can love and remember, and hope to the last.
And for all the base lies that the almanacs hold,
While there's love in the heart, we can never grow old."

"Say it with flowers, say it with eats,
   Say it with kisses, say it with sweets,
   Say it with jewelry, say it with drink,
   But always be careful not to say it with ink!"

Overseas

Australia: *"Cheers!"*

Belgium: *"Santé!"*

Brazil: *"Saúde!"*

China: *"Gan bie!"*

England: *"Cheers!"*

France: *"À votre santé!"*

Guatemala: *"Salud!"*

Germany: *"Prost!"*

Greece: *"Yasas!"*

Holland: *"Proost!"*

Hungary: *"Ege'sze'ge're!"*

India: *"Tulleeho!"*

Ireland: *"Sláinte!"*

Israel: *"Lechaim!"*

Italy: *"Salute!"*

Japan: *"Kampai!"*

Mexico: *"Salud!"*

Philippines: *"Mabuhay!"*

Poland: *"Na Zdrowie!"*

Portugal: *"Tchin tchin!"*

Russia: *"Za vashe zdorovye!"*

Singapore: *"Yam Seng!"*

South Africa: *"Ooogy Wawa!"*

South Korea: *"Gonbae!"*

Sweden: *"Skal!"*

Thailand: *"Chai yo!"*

Ukraine: *"Za vas!"*

ACKNOWLEDGMENTS

Cheers

TO SAY "I STAND ON THE SHOULDERS OF GIANTS" WOULDN'T BE
accurate. It's more like I'm peering over their shoulders trying to catch a glimpse
into their mixing glasses. So elbows bent to the undeniable leaders in the bar field:
Paul Clarke, Dale DeGroff, Ted Haigh, Robert Hess, Gary Regan, Audrey Saunders,
and David Wondrich. Posthumous prost to Jerry Thomas, Harry Craddock,
and W.J. Tarling, who have put so many of these drinks into play as our current
standards.

"Here's mud in your eye!" to our talented bar staff (past and present) at Hearty
Restaurant who have been gracious enough to toss recipes in this mix. Many thanks
to Brendan Reynolds for the Bourbon Blues, Greenside, and La Copa Brasilia.
Thanks to Kris Samiec for the Bison Grass Crusta, Cinnamon Bacon Sangaree, and
Strawberry Pimms Cup and to Carol Donovan for the Breakfast Negroni, Chat Noir,
Rosemary Rhubarb Flip, and Spiced Pisco Sour. Other recipe input came from
Alex Margulies, Austin Reed, and Paul Wacker.

"Here's how!" to the office folk who put it all together; Jane Dystel; and Doug,
Eileen, Kate, and the folks at Agate Surrey. Thanks to James Garrido who acted as
our Jimmy Olsen and was always at the ready—typing, researching, and taste testing.

"Bottoms up!" to everyone who helped with the photos; Bob Moysan, who not
only took the beautiful swizzle stick shots but also talked Steve off the ledge, and
Laurie Proffitt for goodly guidance and glassware. Thank goodness David Mordini

has hoarding issues and stockpiled the swizzle sticks. Thanks to the folks at Architectural Artifacts in Chicago for allowing us to use their awesome space for some of our shots. You should consider having your next big event there... I know a caterer.

"Good health and long life!" to the folks at home, like Quincy and Fernando who watched Nate when the deadline got tight. And thanks to Mike Meyers and his portrayal of the Cat in the Hat for keeping Nate occupied during editing week. And thanks to Nate just 'cause we love you.

Oh, and I almost forgot. Thanks to gin and fresh citrus...you know...'cause we love you too.

Special Thanks

I'd like to specially thank the following bars for having such cool, old neon!

Cafe Ba-Ba-Reeba (p. 96)
2024 N. Halsted St.
Chicago, IL 60614
(773) 935-5000

Dell Rhea's Chicken Basket (p. 19)
645 Joliet Rd.
Willowbrook, IL 60527
(630) 325-0780

The California Clipper Lounge (p. 119)
1002 N. California Ave.
Chicago, IL 60622
(773) 384-2547

Diversey River Bowl (p. 169 and p. 197)
2211 W. Diversey Pkwy.
Chicago, IL 60647
(773) 227-5800

Candlelite (p. 1)
7452 N. Western Ave.
Chicago, IL 60645
(773) 465-0087

Finley Dunne's Tavern (p. 59)
3458 North Lincoln Ave.
Chicago, IL 60657
(773) 477-7311

The Charcoal Oven Restaurant (p. 122)
4400 Golf Rd.
Skokie, IL 60076
(847) 675-8062

Gold Star Bar (p. 21)
1755 W. Division St.
Chicago, IL 60622
(773) 227-8700

Club Lago (p. 154)
331 W. Superior St.
Chicago, IL 60654
(312) 951-2849

Green Mill Cocktail Lounge (p. 41)
4802 N. Broadway St.
Chicago, IL 60640
(773) 878-5552

Petey's Bungalow (p. 52)
4401 W. 95th St.
Oak Lawn, IL 60453
(708) 424-8210

Rainbo Club (p. 39)
1150 N. Damen Ave.
Chicago, IL 60622
(773) 489-5999

Sawa's Old Warsaw Restaurant (p. 29)
9200 West Cermak Rd.
Broadview, IL 60155
(708) 343-9040)

Simon's Tavern (p. 8)
5210 N. Clark St.
Chicago, IL
(773) 878-0894

Uptown Lounge (p. 33)
1136 W. Lawrence Ave.
Chicago, IL 60640
(773) 878-1136

Victory Bar (p. 198)
907 S. Michigan St.
South Bend, IN 46601
(574) 289-5212

Further Reading

How did anyone find information before the internet? I am indebted to the insight and creativity offered at these sites:

A Mountain of Crushed Ice
www.amountainofcrushedice.wordpress.com

About.com
www.about.com

Ardentspirits.com
www.ardentpirits.com
www.gazregan.com

Art of Drink
www.artofdrink.com

Cocktail Chronicles
www.cocktailchronicles.com

Cocktail Database
www.cocktaildb.com

Cocktail Enthusiast
www.cocktailenthusiast.com

Cocktail Spirit with Robert Hess
www.smallscreennetwork.com/show
/cocktail_spirit

Cocktail Times
www.cocktailtimes.com

Cocktail Virgin/Slut
cocktailvirgin.blogspot.com

CocktailDB
www.cocktaildb.com

Diffords Guide
www.diffordsguide.com/index.html

DrinkBoy
www.drinkboy.com

Eatocracy
www.eatocracy.cnn.com

eGullet Forums
www.forums.egullet.org

Epicurious
www.epicurious.com

Esquire Drinks database
www.esquire.com/drinks

Imbibe Magazine
www.imbibemagazine.com

Imbibe Unfiltered
imbibemagazine.blogspot.com

Jeffrey Morgenthaler
www.jeffreymorgenthaler.com

Kaiser Penguin
www.kaiserpenguin.com

Liquorious
www. liquorious.notcot.org

Mixology Monday
www. mixologymonday.com

Oh Gosh!
www. ohgo.sh

The New York Times's Proof
www. proof.blogs.nytimes.com

Rum Dood
www.rumdood.com

Scofflaw's Den
www. scofflawsden.com

Serious Eats
www.seriouseats.com

SLOSHED!
www. sloshed.hyperkinetic.org

Spiritsandcocktails
www. spiritsandcocktails.wordpress.com

The Bitter Truth
www. the-bitter-truth.com

The Chanticleer Society
www. chanticleersociety.org

The Mixoloseum
www. blog.mixoloseum.com

The Pegu Blog
www.killingtime.com/Pegu

Thekitchn.com
www.thekitchn.com

Webtender
www.webtender.com

Wormwood Society
www.wormwoodsociety.org

My single cocktail book shelf long ago spread out and took over the fiction department. I hope you enjoy *The New Old Bar* as much as I've enjoyed reading these:

Café Royal Cocktail Book, by W.J Tarling (Jared Brown publisher 2008)

Drinkology, James Waller *(Stewart, Tabori and Chang, 2003)*

Here's How, compiled by W.C. Whitfield (The Three Mountaineers, Inc., 1942 [out of print])

So Red the Nose, by Sterling North and Carl Kroch (Farrar & Rinehart, 1935 [out of print])

How's Your Drink? by Eric Felten (Agate Surrey, 2009)

Imbibe! by David Wondrich (Perigee Trade, 2007)

Jerry Thomas' Bartenders Guide (various reprints available)

Punch: The Delights (and Dangers) of the Flowing Bowl, by David Wondrich (Perigee Trade, 2010)

The Craft of the Cocktail, by Dale DeGroff (first edition, Clarkson Potter, 2002)

The Joy of Mixology, by Gary Regan (first edition, Clarkson Potter, 2003)

The Savoy Cocktail Book, by Harry Craddock (Pavilion, 2007)

The Ultimate Bar Book, by Mittie Hellmich (Chronicle Books, 2006)

Vintage Cocktails: Authentic Recipes and Illustrations from 1920-1960, by Susan Waggoner Stewart (Tabori and Chang, 2001)

Vintage Spirits and Forgotten Cocktails, by Ted Haigh (Quarry Books, 2009)

INDEX

Drinks appear alphabetically throughout the book. This index compiles the listing by base spirit.